get good® at LIFE

Praise for Get Good® At Life:

"Lee is a wonderful and wise encourager. Pick any double-page spread of this book and it'll improve your life if you put it into action. Accessible, useful, affirming – this is a perfect book for today's busy age. Fostering connections, promoting a routine that works – it's uplifting, time-saving and life-improving. Lee's a great companion on this journey. Let him give you the boost you didn't know you need. You won't regret it."

Paul Kerensa, award-winning comedian and writer
(BBC's *Miranda, Not Going Out, Top Gear*)

"Whether you're a teenager in school, an adult in the workplace or a comedy magician like myself – Lee gives some great advice here to help us all to enjoy and succeed in life. He's a great motivator - I didn't even want to give him a quote!"

John Archer, award-winning comedy magician, *Britain's Got Talent* semi-finalist

"At the end of Lee's book, he suggests we look for the light in a world that can have darkness around every corner. In his own inimitable and Yorkshire way, Lee debunks many motivational myths with well-thought-through, proven, and helpful tips to make our day a better one – and with a smile along the way too."

Peter Roper, best-selling author, award-winning speaker, 'The Family Business Man'

"This book is a brilliant little pick-me-up. Grab a moment, choose a subject, flip to that page, and you will be set up for the day with a positive little nugget."

Michelle Mills Porter aka 'The People Reader'

"If your life is amaaaazing, give this book a miss. Everyone else, fill your boots!"

Dr Andy Cope, aka the 'Dr of Happiness', best-selling author
with over a million books sold

"Less of a book, more an opportunity to eavesdrop into grounded, gritty gems of wisdom that not only provide insight to our present reality but also tools to create a more hopeful future."

Paul McGee, aka 'The SUMO guy'

"In a world of over-used superlatives, Lee Jackson is best described by a word often ignored and unfashionable nowadays. Lee is good. Good at what he does. Good at backing up what he stands for. Good at bringing the best out in others. Everyone would benefit from having a Lee Jackson in their corner. I know I do."

Big Ian Donaghy, speaker/writer

"Get Good® At Life is jam-packed with useful tips, tricks and questions to ask yourself, backed up by references to studies and articles. But what makes this such a great read is his storytelling that gets you laughing, or the songs and movies he mentions that sets you off singing or reminiscing. Put this book in your medicine cabinet rather than the bookshelf. If you're having a bad day, this just might be the medicine you need to get better."

Darren Harris, Paralympian and England blind football team captain

"Down to earth, honest and inspiring."

***Sorted* magazine**

get good® at LIFE

Proven, practical ways to stay connected, motivated and resilient in a complex world

Lee Jackson

ISBN 978-1-9162307-4-3

First published 2023.

Published by Get Good® Books

Original illustrations by Si Smith
Cover design by Andy Ashdown
Editing and typesetting by Candy O'Donovan

Disclaimer:
The information contained within this book is strictly for educational purposes. If you wish to apply ideas contained here, you are taking full responsibility for your actions. Please note that I cannot make any blanket guarantees about the results of the information applied. I share educational and informational resources that are intended to help you. You nevertheless need to know that your ultimate success or failure will be the result of your own efforts, your particular situation, and innumerable other circumstances beyond my knowledge and control. To protect the privacy of certain individuals and organisations some names and identifying details have been changed.

Also by the author:
Get Good® At Presenting
Get Good® At Slides

About the author

I think it's fair to say that Lee Jackson has had a fairly interesting life. He was, for a while, an award-winning DJ and producer in a hip hop band. For over a decade he co-founded and led a charity of youth workers in schools. He is the author of more than a dozen books, a husband, the father of twins and an undersized local league basketball player.

Since 2007 he's been a motivational speaker and presentation coach – working with diverse clients in all sectors as well as Olympic athletes and elected politicians. He is also a past President of the Professional Speaking Association in the UK & Ireland and is one of only twenty-nine people to be awarded the Profesional Speaking Award of Excellence. But with all these things he's done, been and invested in, it all culminates in one thing – communication with, and understanding people. Lee has always been fascinated by people and what makes them tick. Hence this book *Get Good® At Life* – advice from, and reflections on over 25 years working with people from all walks of life.

Lee shares honestly about his life and work as a popular motivational speaker in the personal development industry with top tips on the self-help that works and the myths that don't. He'll steer you through some of the bewildering array of complex self-help myths and offers a down to earth, encouraging and occasionally challenging way to be happier and more fulfilled in everyday life.

With humour, hope, good research and practical solutions Get Good® At Life is the perfect mix of content to survive and thrive in today's world.

You can book Lee to speak at your event via his website:

leejackson.org

Thank you

Thanks to everyone who has helped me with this book. I appreciate all the input and conversations along the way. Special thanks goes to my PSA tribe, my esteemed colleagues Rebecca and Lynda, my masterminders Dave, John, Nathan and Peter. Scott McArthur, Lynne Tapper, Michelle Mills-Porter, Nigel Risner, Big Ian, Steve McDermott, Paul McGee, Barbara Glanz, Andy Cope, Steve Lee, Joan Freeman, Joan Ibbotson, Alan Stevens, Simon Hazeldine, Steve Bustin, John Archer, Nik Keefe, Kriss Akabusi, Kate Ryrie, Sarah Millican, Thomas Møller Jeppesen, Amy Rowlinson, Rob Fry, Paul 'Silky' White, Nicola Adams OBE, Steve Legg, Andy Flannagan, Clare, Rhea, Alex, Lauren, my Mam, my boys - Andy, Duncan, Ian, Baz and many more.

Dedicated to:

Dave Wilki and the Wilki's - Susi, Rosa and Isaac

Joy Marsden and family

And little Miri x

Contents

Introduction

Hello, my name is Lee and I'm a motivational speaker.

Probably quite obvious if you have read the book cover, but I honestly have one of the worst job titles in the world. I only use it because that is what people Google these days. I may well change it as it is a bit weird. At parties, people often don't know how to respond to my job title; they sometimes look at me, step back and with their hands on their hips say, "Go on then – motivate me!" (Maybe dermatologists get shown skin rashes at parties without warning, so I could be getting off lightly.)

Of course the reality is that I can't motivate you, no-one can. It is down to you. I can point things out, encourage and challenge you, but I can't motivate you. I'm not some kind of super-shiny perfect person who never has a bad day and always smiles even when someone has just ran over my foot in their car. I'm maybe a bit big-picture idealistic at times, sure, but also very pragmatic, I'm a realist, and from the north of England too.

I'm all about helping people find the good stuff that can help them be their best. But never from an ivory tower or a six-foot high white horse. I am more likely to be sat next to you on the train or the kerb, listening and occasionally pointing things out. I guess I just love helping people.

Just to be clear as well, I won't be asking you to give up eating everything except roasted macadamia nuts, tell you to drink 17 litres of water a day, or ask you to hold your breath for seven minutes on a frozen lake while doing headstand on an organic satsuma. I'm not about strange theories and odd ideas, but the practical stuff and inspiring stories that could make a real difference, busting a few myths of the personal development industry along the way.

What I'll tell you in this book is based on my experience and my work, I'll help you get the right stuff into your head and your heart so you can do the work, to get the results that you really can achieve. My reason for doing all the work I do is simple. Life and work is not an easy place sometimes, and most of us have to do things we don't like or are hard, it is just something that we have to go through, to get somewhere else, like the career we want or the life you're excited by.

Whatever your view on life or even what happens after life, we only have a short time here - so we may as well give it our best shot. It just makes sense.

> Do what you can, with what you have, where you are.
>
> ***Theodore Roosevelt***

1

The power of connection

DEEP DIVE

LEGO® bricks

Some of the first words I ever published were these:

"Life... is fundamentally, all about the 3Rs: relationships, relationships, relationships..."

A quarter of a century later, I still stand by this statement. Connection is life.

Going back to basics, we cannot deny that life is ultimately about the relationships we have. The relationships we have with others, ourself, at work and the world around us. As much as we might like to think this is not true and it is all about me, my carefully written goals and my Instagram likes, it isn't really.

Without connection, we wouldn't get very far, or, achieve very much. And even if we do achieve, who would we share those successes with?

The 3Rs statement above wasn't written by a social media guru, a hermit or a monk – it was written by my joiner, Rob. It turned out he had written these words in a haze of caffeine in the middle of the night, while looking after his toddlers and applying for a new job in youth work in his 20s.

But even so, the words still ring true. I guess they have, over the years, become one of my key messages. In fact, a series of talks based on that statement formed the basis of my first paid speaking gigs.

Over the years, of course, my thoughts have developed and changed, but still the fact remains, I believe that prioritising our relationships and connections with others makes for a happier, healthier and more fruitful life.

Think about it – everything we do involves connecting. When we go to a shop and buy something, we have a brief connection with the person behind the counter. We don't have to plait their hair or sit cross-legged making daisy chains with them, but you know that the connection acts as a spoonful of sugar and will help the medicine go down.

Work is full of connections; at home it's the same. What is more important than relationships? Our relationships with our partner, children, family and friends are the most important things in our lives.

I like the phrase, 'The main thing, is to keep the main thing, the main thing'. The main thing for humans is: connection. Nothing is more important, and nothing comes close to matching it.

I have lost count of the number of people I know who have talked about reshaping their lives away from non-stop work to re-prioritising things and putting their family or, often, their health first. Putting relationships first in our lives means that everything else kind of falls into its rightful place.

Don't panic – we aren't talking about perfection here, I fail, we all fail. I get things wrong; I try not to, but it happens. That is life (more on that later). But even though I fail occasionally, I still like to keep this value in the forefront of my mind.

We are like LEGO® bricks.

The brick itself is brilliantly designed and has been engineered for many years to fit well with others. LEGO® told me in an interview that they use up to 25 different types of plastic in their designs, and now their trees are made of soya. Anyway, I digress.

A single brick might be a piece of engineering mastery, but it's kind of sad on its own. The whole idea of LEGO® bricks are that they are meant to connect with others.

They connect to create.

They connect to support.

They are still individuals, but they have a higher purpose which is only ever realised when they connect with others.

The engineers at LEGO® say that their bricks differ from the generic copies that we see because they have spent years working on what they call 'clutch power'. That is the power that the brick design has: its power to connect, how strong that connection is and how long the connection will last. The bricks are designed to last over 25 years. And as a Dad I can say that it's true – my daughters had a big bucket of Lego® and Duplo® bricks; almost 25 years later, that that bucket of bricks is still enjoyed by kids who visit our house.

Some connections are fleeting, some are designed to last well over 25 years.

In the last few years it has been great to hear people talking more openly about kindness, connection, honesty and vulnerability. These can be sadly lacking in the cut and thrust of the highly competitive personal and professional development industry. If we're not careful we can be duped into thinking that developing ourselves is all about just that – ourselves.

Criminal behaviour

To move towards better and deeper connection with people, we firstly need to develop a greater sense of honesty – with ourselves and others.

In one of my first jobs I worked in a law court (I thought I'd start as a criminal and work my way up). Aged 21, as a pre-IT admin assistant, I basically shuffled paper from one side of my desk to the other and then went home. There was very little stress, but I knew it wasn't for me, especially when I heard 25-year-olds in the office talking openly about their retirement! It paid the bills for a while, and I learnt a lot there, watching people and their quirky ways and routines.

In the mornings there used to be a ritual that made me smile: it was the 'let's say good morning to everyone in an open office' routine. It was the most stereotypically British thing ever. Everyone used to say, "Morning, how are you?" It was nice, but no one ever replied honestly or even listened for a reply. "Yeah, fine thanks", "Not bad", or "Fair to middling" (it was Yorkshire after all) were the only responses. Some people even answered the question when they hadn't even been asked.

On my cheekier days, I loved giving people a bit more information than they wanted: "Well, I feel a bit tired, actually, and I'm concerned about the deforestation of the Amazon. Oh, and I think my dog has fleas."' You have never seen people run so fast.

Years later, when I was a youth worker, I remember a high-flying and 'influential' youth worker announcing to me that he had chosen me as his friend. We had a couple of coffees together, after which he only talked to me when he needed something.

We didn't keep in touch. There was no real connection there.

People sometimes disappoint. Sometimes our relationships and connections are transactional: the 'You do this for me and I do this for you' type of thing. This can be a bit cold, but it is quite practical for certain things too. The real sadness is when people only have transactional connections and relationships and nothing any deeper or lasting.

I've known people over the years who genuinely thought that they could survive on their own, that they didn't need anybody. They live on their own, they do their own thing, and barely have any real connections at all. Sadly some of these people have developed health problems and ended up struggling through life.

DJ

I still DJ for friends occasionally: weddings and parties – that kind of thing. It used to be a big part of my life; now I just do it for fun. But as time has moved on people expect a DJ at a party, not to be a DJ, but to be a jukebox. People come up to me with a list of songs they want me to play. They sometimes want to send me a song or share their killer playlist of their favourite songs, often the songs they love to sing in the car.

Often, however, the songs we like the most are actually terrible for DJs at parties. Our favourite song may even empty the dance floor.

A DJ is not a jukebox and neither is a connection or a friend, if we treat people like that we will forever stay in one-sided transactional relationships.

> “Football was invented because men have got nothing to say to their mates.”
>
> **Ben Elton**

A bit more real

We will meet some amazing and slightly odd people in our travels, I quite like that: people will come and go. Some connections we make will disappear and some will get deeper.

What is important, however, is to get a bit more real with some people in our lives – and certainly stop papering over the cracks. To tell our stuff to someone, but not to everyone.

There is a fine line between being honest and becoming a constant whinger. We have to find the balance. And I think that exists in choosing who to be really honest with. Talk to some, just don't talk to everyone. We have to unload on some people but don't over-share with everyone. Choose your friends who you can share with carefully. But do choose some and ask their permission, then do the same for them.

We can't do life alone; even if we are single and live alone, we aren't alone, and shouldn't aim to be. I knew someone; one of my friends warned me about how destructive and angry they could be. I hadn't seem that side of them, but they were right, sadly. I watched, that person, over a couple of years chip away at every connection they had made. Their world got smaller and smaller, then they started rejecting help and advice, until eventually they gradually disappeared from everyones life and became alone and bereft, in every sense. It was a reminder to all just how important connection is.

Yes people are difficult sometimes, yes, people can be annoying and hard to deal with, but nothing replaces that real connection and true friendship. I have certainly learned that the hard way.

Before we move on, a quick word about men, a demographic I feel very qualified to speak about.

Men, in my opinion, are often so much worse at having better or deeper connections. My observation is that my wife will speak for hours with her friends in coffee shops or on video calls, sharing deeply, often looking at them while speaking, but some men I know often just grunt or talk about work and football, at least initially.

Small talk is important for creating rapport and checking in with people. The problem is that men, particularly, often never get beyond the banter or small talk. Deep down they can be shallow.

And sadly the figures on mental heath problems and suicide, in young men particularly, are a sad reflection on how men think that they have to keep all feelings inside and not share their thoughts and struggles with other men.

A few years ago I was part of an exercise class. We'd turn up twice a week to run and do exercises around the local park. There was lots of fun, mutual exhaustion and banter in the group. We even went out for a drink occasionally to replace the calories we had spent the previous hour losing. 'Jack' turned up regularly. He'd drive up in a new car every other week, each more lavish than the last – his business seemed to be doing well. People looked up to him, he was fun to have around too.

One week, we got a text out of the blue saying that 'Jack' had killed himself. A few days later, we stood in silence at his funeral, stunned at what had happened, and watched his family trying to make sense of it all. That was a tough day.

I'm not saying that he didn't have any friends, but I often wonder, if he'd been able to talk to some good mates a few months earlier about his worries and his problems, whether he'd still be here now trying to do press-ups on a bench in the park, with me going bright red next to him. In the world's eyes he had it all, but our perceptions of success and happiness can often be shallow at best and totally wrong at worst.

Everyone is different of course: some love to overshare, some are very closed and private. I don't mind that, as we have all been brought up differently or have different personality types. But the bigger issue is that keeping everything inside and never sharing where we are at, is simply not good for us.

Humans make terrible pressure cookers. People are in our life for a reason.

By the way – if you want a man to open up more, make sure you are not staring at him when talking to him. If he is looking into the distance, stand or sit next to him and face the same way. A car journey, doing a task together or a long walk, might be a helpful setting; it's the direct eye contact that freaks many men out. Many don't know how to process it. They may talk eventually but not if you stare at them. Take a road trip or a walk, or put up an Ikea wardrobe (other brands of wardrobe are available).

Health

We all know that having good relationships are important to us. Connecting well is good for our personal life, our work life, but do you know that relationships are also good for our health?

There are peer-reviewed scientific studies to back this up too. Just one *New York Times* article[1] cites several.

- In Australia[2] they studied 1,500 70-year-olds and found that those with a good friendship group were 22% less likely to die during the ten-year study.
- In Sweden[3] they studied middle-aged men and found that a lack of relational support was as harmful to their health as smoking.
- In a study[4] of breast cancer patients, those without close friendship and support were twice as likely to die than those with close support.

In 2011 there was a large earthquake and tsunami originating in Japan. Over 15,000 people were killed, and over 130,000 people displaced – a terrible event. A study[5] was later carried out which found that those who became more isolated because of the quake and its after-effects, got more ill and died younger. Relational isolation affected both their quality and length of life.

Connecting with others well isn't just 'nice' or 'cute' or an 'add-on' – it is literally good for us. Let's not forget that in these busy times.

1 https://www.nytimes.com/guides/smarterliving/how-to-be-a-better-friend
2 https://jech.bmj.com/content/59/7/574
3 https://journals.lww.com/psychosomaticmedicine/Abstract/1993/01000/Lack_of_social_support_and_incidence_of_coronary.7.aspx
4 https://ascopubs.org/doi/abs/10.1200/JCO.2005.04.2846
5 https://europepmc.org/article/MED/35410023

Social media actually taught me something…[6]

Did you know that there are 12 levels of friendship in Arabic?

1. ***Zameel*** – someone you have a nodding acquaintance with
2. ***Jalees*** – someone you're comfortable sitting with for a while
3. ***Sameer*** – someone you have a good conversation with
4. ***Nadeem*** – a drinking companion (tea/coffee/wine/beer) that you might call when you're free
5. ***Sahib*** – someone who's genuinely concerned for your wellbeing
6. ***Rafeeq*** – someone you can depend upon; you might go on holiday with them
7. ***Sadeeq*** – a true friend, someone who doesn't befriend you for an ulterior motive
8. ***Khaleel*** – an more intimate friend, someone whose presence makes you happy
9. ***Anees*** – someone you're really comfortable with
10. ***Najiyy*** – a confidant, someone you trust deeply
11. ***Safiyy*** – a best friend, someone you've chosen over others
12. ***Qareen*** – someone who's inseparable from you. You know how they think (and vice versa)

Most of our friends are level 5 or below, and many of us don't have a single level 10+ friend. Food for thought, eh?

Life can be challenging. 'Stuff' happens to us all; we need connection, friendship, support, good input and – unfashionably – an occasional kick to help us to thrive.

The ultimate test of whether someone is a good friend or not is fairly simple. Would they drive you to the airport if you asked them?

---

6 Source: https://threadreaderapp.com/thread/1402681643714985984.html
Used with the kind permission of Taariq Ismail.

Fuel

In 1944 Britain were losing the Second World War. The big push known as D-Day was being planned, but they had a problem – they might run out of fuel.

Pause now and watch this short four-minute video for more on that and why we can learn from it: https://bit.ly/GetGoodDDayVideo

My friend Steve told me this story years ago. It is so good. Even the greatest feat of World War II needed fuel to keep it going. It needed a pipeline to feed it.

We're not designed to do life, and work alone.

Let's just kill that sacred cow right now: there is no such thing as solo success.

Dig deeper into your heroes and you will realise that everyone has a team around them in some way. Get a team around you to give you fuel.

Start small, but start soon.

- Who could be on your team?
- Who could help you on your journey?
- Who is in your circle of influence?
- Who do you have around you right now you can be grateful for?

In my deeper friendship accountability group there is a church minister, a community worker, me, and a dentist. We are all different but we meet together for one purpose, deeper accountable friendship and connection. True friendships are a little deeper than normal. Good relationships aren't usually made quickly (some are of course); generally they take time to develop, like a fine wine. We have had this group for over 20 years now. It has been worth the investment; it is one of the best things I have ever done.

Learn to recognise and evaluate who is on your team. You may have friends that you've known for years, you may have friends that aren't good for you. Always a tough one that, but be honest with yourself here.

You may have friends that serve a particular purpose for you, the one that is a good listener, the one who you can be silly with and the one with the work and relationships wisdom.

Connect more, connect better, connect more deeply.

Tips for connection

- To connect more, be yourself. Be kind, smile, use people's names, listen more, listen well, be interested.
- Don't look over someone's shoulder while talking to them to find something more interesting to do. I see this often at networking events.
- People love handwritten thank-you cards.
- Put your phone face down or switch it off when meeting someone.

Little things like this all add up to greater connection. Greater LEGO® brick 'clutch power'.

> “You can make more friends in two months by becoming interested in other people, than you can in two years by trying to get other people interested in you.”
>
> ***Dale Carnegie***[7]

7 *How to Win Friends and Influence People* (1936)

The awkward truth about materialism

Don't let 'things' get in the way or distract you. It is enjoyable to have nice things, but let's be honest – they don't give us happiness or fulfilment. I knew a guy who was earning a lot of money in professional services. He said that he filled up his car with gadgets and expensive shopping every Saturday, as he went out and spent what he'd earned working hard.

One Saturday, he opened the boot of his posh car to put in that day's shopping but it was still full of the stuff he'd put there the week before. It made him stop and think. He eventually left his job and did community work abroad. That is not everyone's path, but for him he knew he had to change his life, for his own sake. He chose purpose over things.

In the best-selling book on depression and anxiety, *Lost Connections*, Johann Hari interviews Tim Kasser, an associate professor of psychology. In his research[8] Professor Kasser looked at values and initially studied groups of students, moving on to the various aged citizens of Rochester, New York. He noticed in the students that the more they pursued materialistic things, the less happy they were. Thinking surely this is just an issue for younger people he extended his study out. But he still found this inconvenient truth: "A strong desire for materialistic pursuits… decreased the quality of their daily experience". And as Hari says, "They experienced less joy and more despair".

Wow.

Now I know I sound very hippy-ish here, and I'm fully aware that I am writing this on a nice Macbook with my iPhone lying next to me. But still, we can't ignore this stuff. Connection and intrinsic pursuits (more on that later) make us happier.

When people visit their elderly parents with delirium or dementia, they often don't know who they are, but they quite often want to hold their visitor's hand. They don't lie there worrying whether their TV is the latest model. They want to feel loved.

---

8 *The High Price of Materialism* (2003)

Just like a LEGO® brick, we are designed for connection. We need it. We don't need another wardrobe of designer gear.

Even so, I still see so many people vehemently pursuing this endless materialistic dream. I have heard seminars about making big goals for posh cars, houses and jet-set lifestyles. I was in a networking meeting once where people resorted to comparing their gold and platinum international flight club cards. This is sometimes known in my line of work as 'willy waving'.

I wonder if sometimes they mention this stuff out loud to keep themselves playing the game. Because pursuing this type of goal is all-consuming. It is cathartic in the extreme. It takes up our time and effort. The adverts will never stop; Amazon, like Netflix, cannot be completed, and the Instagram lifestyle tips from someone on a green screen in a damp basement flat will probably never end either.

It is maybe the big lie that we have all been sold every day. 280 times a day.

Mental heath problems and unhappiness are the great leveller, a bit like Covid-19 was. No matter how much money we had or what car we drove, we were all at risk of being infected. We can all be unhappy too.

Even though we all know deep down that we need connection to thrive, why do we continue to try and find happiness in places that have been proven not to work? I love people, and I really hate to see them making the same mistakes again and again. But it is all part of life's rich tapestry, as they say. And anyway, I know that unless someone is ready, we can't teach them anything.

A few connection challenges

- Arrange a meeting with someone you work with, for no reason other than to talk to them. Resist the temptation to get something from them. Just listen.
- To a very select few, try to answer more honestly when they ask you how you are.
- Talk to your good friends about your weaknesses as well, so they know you are not superhuman and you want a real relationship with them.
- When you ask people how they are, wait to hear an answer.
- Make that phone call you keep putting off.
- Instead of buying something online that you may not need, spend that money on taking someone important to you out for a meal or a day out, tell them not to bring any money.
- When you are 'filling up' your diary, remember the importance of connection. Build in a few minutes for yourself and relational time too.

QUICK WINS

The cleaner

I was once speaking at a posh venue in London. In the break I saw the cleaner who had closed the loo for cleaning. He looked stressed and hassled. Anyway, we got talking. He told me it was his birthday that day, but he had to work and wasn't really celebrating it at all as his friends were not there in London. So when I went back to my training room I gathered up some sweets and chocolate and wrote him a card (I always try to carry thank-you cards). I left that cleaner a little birthday parcel – outside the men's toilet! I never saw him again, but I hope that I helped him that day. It also had the bonus side effect of making me feel good, despite a long tiring day on my feet.

Look out for these little opportunities: make someone's day, with a simple act of connection.

Coffee

A few days after a family bereavement I spent 90 minutes talking to a good friend in a coffee shop. I didn't realise I could talk about it for well over an hour, but I did, and it was helpful to get my thoughts in order. He is a good man.

Never underestimate the power of true connection. Value the connections you have over the false feeling that we need to hustle all the time. The addictive feeling of busyness rarely ever goes away in working life.

Training

The two most important things we have to handle in life are probably relationships and parenthood, and we don't get trained for either of them.

Most people get more training on how to lift a box at work than how to be a healthy parent or partner. Train yourself through watching, reading and sharing.

Names

I used to work a day a week in one of the toughest schools in the country, it was the second worst on the national school league tables. With some others, I ran a session on the importance of names. A 12-year-old lad put his hand up and said, "My Dad calls me a*sewipe. Nothing else, just that."

So we asked him his real name. It was David, so we said, "I tell you what, we'll call you David instead." He turned up every week after that and became our little helper.

Learn and use people's names, there is no sweeter sound to anyone than the sound of their own name.[9]

9 A paraphrase of Dale Carnegie's phrase from the 1920s

Medics

According to a senior medic that I interviewed, he was very concerned that in the last few years he is now seeing more and more highly qualified 23-year-old medics who are really struggling with their 'bedside manner' skills, both with patients and socially.

I asked him why he thought this was happening. He was convinced that excessive social media has lowered these young doctors' one-to-one communication skills – so his organisation now trains them on these basic skills too.

Obviously this is not serious or deep research on my part, but I trust this person and I was shocked at his comments. Who in your workplace or organisation might need some training to connect better?

Thank you

A well placed and specific thank you goes a long way. If you want to make a real difference, thank someone in front of their peers or their boss. Don't be vague either, saying, "They were nice" – say, "I loved the way they helped me with..." Specific thank-yous and feedback work very well at work and in everyday life.

Expectations

Don't expect praise from anyone.

Change the atmosphere where you are by giving praise or just a smile to others instead.

Ubuntu

In the 2008 season the winning NBA team the Boston Celtics fully embraced the idea of 'Ubuntu' - championed in Africa and made famous by Desmond Tutu.

Ubuntu means 'humanity' and is often translated as 'I am because we are'. The Celtics ascribe their success to this concept and the values it instilled in them.[10] Read more in the links in the footnotes.

10 https://celticswire.usatoday.com/lists/nba-boston-celtics-ubuntu-origin/
https://byrslf.co/i-am-because-we-are-how-the-concept-of-ubuntu-triggered-the-biggest-turnaround-in-nba-history-2ddbfe230f96

Home video

I spent some time recently digitising some of our old family videos from the VHS and Camcorder days. Seeing the old footage was great, but the best bit was my Mum and Dad smiling at each other and enjoying each other's company on camera, rather than the endless hours of scenery or the cottage we stayed in once.

2

The pain of disconnection

DEEP DIVE

I have extolled the importance of connection and relationships.

But what do we do when we come across awkward, challenging or even, downright difficult people?

Or to use the LEGO® brick analogy – yes, they and we are designed for connection, but eventually we will step on a brick in our bare feet. That pain is the same the world over. It hurts. A lot.

I have learnt some of the lessons here through trial and error, sweat, stress, and occasionally through tightly gritted teeth – while being fully aware that I might, at times, have been a difficult person too.

So without sounding like I have it all sorted, here are some stories and tips for dealing with life's relational stones in our shoe.

With people, I have learnt that:

- We can't control them (wouldn't that be easier!)
- We can't teach them, unless they're ready and willing to learn
- They'll do things that annoy us or we don't understand
- We are all different

- Our happiness should not be reliant on other people's attitude or opinion of us
- Sometimes we have to shake our head, shrug, blow out our cheeks, shake the dust from our feet and move on. And no, that isn't as easy as it sounds. Annoying, that.

Not ready to learn

A few years ago I was delivering a four-hour speaking skills workshop with seventy 17-year-olds. What can I say? I like a challenge. From the off, one of the teenagers kept saying out loud, "I don't like it, I'm no good at it, I can't do it".

Throughout the afternoon, to help them to learn, I used my full repertoire. I smiled a lot, encouraged them publicly and privately and of course occasionally nudged them into action too. After four hours, I felt that I had used my full arsenal of people skills with this one person to get them to engage. They just ignored it all – with, "I'm not good at this", "I can't do it" constantly thrown back at me and the really supportive group they were part of. Driving home I felt flat, tired. I felt like I had failed. So that night I wrote down a few things that I had learnt from that sad situation.

Firstly, I didn't really know them; their background was probably very challenging and maybe they had never been encouraged, ever. What words might have been spoken over them? I do wish the organiser had warned me though. Lesson learnt there for the future – I ask loads more questions now.

Secondly, being a human is just challenging sometimes, very challenging.

Thirdly, some people's self-talk (the messages that play on repeat in our heads, usually just behind our consciousness) is so constantly negative that life virtually stops for them. They only exist. It's genuinely grim.

Fourthly, I'd done the right thing: I'd smiled at them and encouraged them, because they still needed to know that they are valued, that they can do something and be someone.

And finally, being constantly negative gets you nowhere.

They tried nothing.

They gained nothing.

At the beginning of the day, this person's feedback sheet showed 1 out of 10 for speaking confidence; at the end of the day it was still 1 out of 10. I averaged 50-60% improvement that day. I'm not even sure that the hard stats helped the penny drop, but for their sake I hope it drops at some point. Some people endure lives that are stuck in a rut and, to paraphrase Henry David Thoreau, many go to the grave with their potential still locked up inside them.

Sometimes it is because they are hurt, afraid of stepping up, or standing out, they over-think stuff or they just aren't willing to engage. People are complex; we all have different starting points and it is always nature and nurture, never just one or the other.

Even after a tough day like that, this still is one reason I do my job, because I don't want anyone to not have the confidence to be the person they were born to be.

On the whole, people are just trying their best with what they have - their current attitude, their level of education, their learned life skills and their current amount of self-awareness. So I try hard to think the best of people and be as kind as possible.

Occasionally we need to stand our ground and hold fast with some people, but most of the time it does help to simply listen more and be kinder.

Even to the most challenging people we meet.

Check their filing cabinet

In one of my first jobs, I was feeling confused because I just couldn't get through to a person I was working with. So I went to see my mentor, Mike, and shared my frustration and he told me: "Lee, they just don't have that file in their filing cabinet".

We cannot help or teach someone something new unless they have that 'file' in their filing cabinet (or folder on their desktop or app on their phone). They just don't have anywhere to store and file away that new information, and their view of themselves, their self-esteem, is one of the biggest factors.

I was booked to do a workshop a while back and when I arrived I realised that the delegates were not ready for my 'motivational session', so there and then I changed my session to one about self-esteem. I made it all about their true value, and once I had set the scene and built them up a little I was able to give them some tips to help them move forward. I had started to build that file for their filing cabinet.

So when honestly you feel like you are banging your head against a brick wall with someone, stop and think, have they got that file in their filing cabinet? If they haven't, change your tack, change your approach and start to build that file for them.

But what happens if people just don't like us?

For a few months I was in a sports team where some of the players just seemed to hate me. I left in the end because of it. I had helped them, been out with them for beers, played hard, paid my dues, been a faithful member of the team but, for whatever reason, some of them just seemed to hate me. They loved it when I messed up or got fouled – it was weird. I had become a Dad too during that time, and told them, all excited in a new Dad kind of way. They just shrugged and told me what a nightmare teething is. Cheers lads. After I had left the team, I played against them with another one. They still heckled me and were delighted when we lost the match.

Honestly. Some people we will never connect with, no matter what we do. Learn from it, shrug, smile and move on. There is nothing I could have done there. It was definitely them and not me. I had tried everything. Ah well.

We are all impressionists

One of my favourite speakers is Barbara Glanz.[11] As a customer service expert, she talks about how little things can make a big difference – and how helping someone and going the extra mile can mean more profit as well as a better life.

Barbara has one of the only email newsletters that I actually read. She shares very honestly about her family life, her work, what she's learning and always includes a few snippets of wisdom.

She shared something from one of her talks recently which is a little diagram with a minus (-) on the left, a zero (0) in the middle and plus (+) on the right.

- 0 +

She talks about, how, when we meet people, we have a choice.

A choice to leave an interaction with:

- (a negative)

0 (a business level interaction)

+ (a human level connection)

We leave a mark or an impression in most of our interactions throughout the day – people we speak to on the phone, people in shops, family, friends and even people that we just bump into in thestreet. Larry David has made a long-running improvised comedy show out of his awkward encounters with others on the famous *Curb Your Enthusiasm*.

The impressions that we make are sometimes very light and fleeting: "That guy just cut me up", "They were a bit rude" etc.

11 https://barbaraglanz.com

Sometimes, however, we leave a bigger mark, a Sharpie® marker kind of mark. Sometimes we even leave a tattoo or, sadly, a scar.

It's unrealistic to think that we travel on the earth for however long we've got without leaving any marks. The sobering reality is that we leave impressions all the time. So maybe, as we prioritise and understand the power of connection, this is how we can get to know our impact on the world and on others.

We can become grateful to have the privilege to leave an impression on others. I'm sure it won't always be positive, but we can try to leave, as Barbara says, a 'human level connection'. Try to see the value and gold in people, to bring out the best in them, to speak truth in love and bring light into dark places.

My favourite audiences as a speaker are probably the slightly stressed-out and reluctant ones. I feel I work well in that situation; I want to help them and bring something for them or out of them that will give them life.

So without beating yourself up, take stock of some of the impressions and marks you've left on people. How could you leave a more positive mark tomorrow on somebody that you meet? How can you serve them better?

Today, I was struggling to write – so I took a break and went to my local post office to send some parcels and found out that they are closing. The team behind the counter have been really good-humoured, efficient and great to deal with over the last few years. I told them I'll miss them. I'll have a card and a small present for them nearer the time too. Today, they looked a little worried. They're losing their jobs. As the shop was fairly quiet, I had a chance to listen to them for a couple of minutes. I think I left a positive mark, and helped them, just briefly, in their time of uncertainty. It only took two more minutes out of my day and a small box of chocolates.

Next time you interact with your colleagues and contacts, can you leave a '0' or a '+', a positive mark, a kinder impression?

Hotel break(down)

We were staying in a seaside hotel recently for a weekend break, but there were a few problems with the room. So I went to the hotel reception to let them know. They seemed very open to helping us have a great stay. I approached the reception desk and spoke to a woman in her early 20s. I spoke to her calmly and told her about the problems with our room.

Quietly, this lady started to well up. When I asked if she was OK, she ran out crying. I waited around for a few minutes, but she didn't come back and so I quietly went back to our room. The next day she saw me walk in to reception and she looked nervous. I noticed this and so I broke the ice and we chatted. I listened for a couple of minutes, as she opened up about the tough week she'd had with her family.

We talked, I said I was sorry for the tough week she'd had, we smiled, fist-bumped and I left. Hopefully I left her in a better state than she was.

Social media ranting

I've noticed a new trend. Some people post on their social media how they've just met someone and something odd happened.

Maybe the person they met was a bit rude. People can be. Maybe they didn't have the budget to buy our services. BUT – don't jeopardise your connections by using social media badly.

If something has happened talk to someone - don't just put it online.

Stuff like this happens, but what I don't get is: why don't people realise that the person they're talking about will probably see that post? I reckon most will. Imagine seeing a negative post about yourself an hour after meeting someone. Not good. Even those Instagram and Tiktok videos with a sarcastic song saying, "I work (insert swear word here) hard to do my job" are a bit odd.

We do, have to have boundaries and cut ourselves off from people occasionally but honestly - don't burn your bridges for a rant. People who I've known for years and are very different to me and have different opinions have sometimes become my friends, colleagues and even paying clients.

Don't burn bridges in private or public for the sake of a a few clicks on a social media post. Call a friend, get it off your chest, and file it all in that 'ah well that was weird' box in your head, shrug, and move along – nothing to see here.

Truth versus opinions

I love lemon curd. This lemony sweet spread is perfect with buttery white toast. I've loved it since my Nanna gave it to me as a kid. I would live on the stuff, if I could get away with it.

But maybe you can't stand lemon curd, maybe as much as I can't stand opera.[12] That's OK. It's an opinion, a preference. Maybe for you, lemon curd is disgusting. That doesn't make it disgusting for everyone.

Everyone has opinions, some of them are pretty strong.

We can have opinions that are both strong and wrong.

Some opinions are wrong and could not be proven in a court of law. But truth is truth, no matter what anyone says. Some things are true and do not move. Holding on to some truths is good for us - we are not designed to see the whole world shifting and moving and changing all the time. We need fixed points and, so, truths are helpful.

Learning to distinguish between truths and opinions – especially the ones we'd like to be true – is real maturity.

We can search Youtube to try to prove our opinions are true, of course, but we can easily end up using incorrect or false sources. Life is trickier in this way now.

There are things even in this book that I thought I'd say, but then investigated them more and it proved that I was either wrong or that they were inconclusive – a grey area. I am OK with being proven wrong, and

12 Don't panic – I am exaggerating for comedy effect, but I have never understood why they are always bursting into song, particularly, it seems, when they are dying!

I quite like some grey areas, including my hair. That is why we all need more wisdom in our lives, and it develops at various ages, not necessarily in old age.

Knowledge is good – truth and wisdom are even better.

Some people are challenging to get on with because of their strong opinions. I have tried to debate with people like this, but rarely do people move from their entrenched opinionated positions. So, often, I like to adopt the 'let's agree to disagree' approach at that point. No argument about lemon curd is worth ruining a valued relationship over, like we saw here in the UK over Brexit in 2016 and in the US over a certain President or two.

Acceptance and agreement

I've always been a bit of a people-watcher – I can sit and watch people come and go in airports, train stations and coffee shops for ages. I notice funny things like the panic that some people have boarding an aeroplane, desperately looking for a seat like their life depended on it. Now I've been on a quite a few flights in my life and I've never in all that time seen the cabin crew send people back out to the airport because they are full. They do overbook planes, but they always count the seats before offering a boarding pass. Yet still, people are panicking for a seat as they think there won't be enough.

So, when I see quirky or interesting things, I sometimes forget them, some I note down and speak on stage about, some I'm wrong about, but some little things really stick in my mind and I give them more thought and chat to mates about what I've noticed.

This is one of those issues I've discussed a fair bit recently, though it is a bit controversial.

I think we have a growing problem in our society. A new problem. And that is that it's becoming almost impossible these days to have a genuine disagreement and debate with others.

It's becoming almost impossible to disagree politely with people.

Whether online or offline, this is becoming a problem.

Online, it's a problem because of internet trolls, bots, aggressive agenda-driven social media commenting, and people not really understanding how debate works. My main concern, though, is that often this can, and does sometimes spill over into real life too.

Fundamentally I think disagreeing with someone is a good thing and it is part of a healthy life and society. It's a skill that we should learn and use well.

But more and more I see that people just don't like others having different views. I think it's a real shame. I blame Brexit, again. Well, kind of. Before the vote here in the UK social media became people 'broadcasting' what they thought and slagging others off who disagreed with them, via text, gif or meme. There was very little sensible debate – it ended up being just people being rude to each other and then getting blocked, reported or 'unfriended'. And just like the miners' strike in the 80s, families have broken up because of it in the UK.

During that period, I did manage to have some debates with people in person, but often people just gave their best tabloid press answer and didn't listen to the other side of the story. We were all guilty of that.

I'm genuinely concerned though. Let's hope that debate and healthy disagreement can stay alive. It is vital.

In order to prepare for real life we need to meet and discuss big issues with people that hold the opposite view from us. It is just how we do it that is key.

We can still accept people fully without agreeing with everything little thing they believe in.

The difference between acceptance and agreement is crucial.

I will accept and be respectful to everyone, even certain politicians, but I won't necessarily agree with them. That's called being sensible, people-focused and respectful. It is being a civil person, it is valuing people.

There are issues that have become no-go areas today and some people just don't know how to chat to someone who doesn't hold the same opinion as them.

Here are three things that may help us all to keep debate and respectful disagreement as part of our life, and remove some of the drama along the way.

1. Remember that on social media, email and on the phone, there is (usually) a real person at the other end.
2. When people are giving their views to you, listen to what they are saying, don't just think of, or web search for, your next killer statement to shoot them down with.
3. Remember that our goal in life isn't to win all arguments and have no friends.

The distinction between acceptance and agreement has really helped me to connect with, and maintain relationships with family, friends and colleagues.

I'm also working hard to be a person who is not easily offended. I try to value everyone including those who believe different things to me.

I will and do fail, but I'll keep trying because I know I don't have to fully agree with someone to fully accept and value them.

Yes, even hardcore conspiracy theorists…

Flat earth

I can prove that the earth is round. I'm not going to go into it here. But it is. That is a fact. But I have met people who believe that it is flat. Fair enough, that is up to them. It is, as is often said, a free country.

Some conspiracy theories may well be true, I guess we will never know. They love that, by the way.

Maybe we all need to believe one harmless conspiracy theory just to say we have one. For instance, the conspiracy theory that whatever airport security queue you join, the other one will probably go faster. If we each have a harmless one like this, it may well help us understand why people can dive headfirst into these and they take over their lives.

It is good to understand a few key things on these theories, as it helps us understand others, ourselves and our brains better.

First up is the power of confirmation bias, or 'fixation'.

Confirmation bias is a psychological term that means that people tend to search for, and often cherry-pick information that helps to confirm their beliefs or biases – ie, if we believe that the earth is flat, we can easily flood our life with articles, books and videos from people who also believe the same, therefore confirming our bias.

The term has got a little overused and mildly controversial in the last few years, so some now prefer the term 'fixation'. If we think that my hometown team Middlesbrough FC are the best football team in the world (no one ever has by the way), we can fixate on them and fill our lives with red and white and photos of the Riverside stadium. We all do this to an extent with things. But the danger is in the fixation. We have all probably met or known family or friends that have gone down the Youtube rabbit hole and emerged a few weeks later with a whole new set of beliefs.

During the height of the Covid lockdown, when conspiracy theories were rife, I was queuing up with many others outside our local supermarket to get some essentials. Behind me in the queue was a very grumpy guy who was grumbling and mumbling, getting louder and louder. After five whole earth minutes in the queue I heard him say:

"It's all a hoax this."

"It's a lie."

"The government has made this up!"

"Why do we have to queue?"

"It's disgusting."

At this point a lot of people were dying and the hospitals were full. But this guy kept going on and on, not knowing if anyone in the long queue had just lost a loved one. So eventually, after seeing the twenty people near me eye-rolling each other, I took the bait. I turned to him and said, "So you think this is all fake, then?" He nodded. "How did you find out?" I asked, "Youtube", he said. We chatted and he freely spouted forth his opinions.

After a few minutes, I asked him, "Do you think 9-11 was a hoax as well?" "Oh yeah, definitely", he replied. I cheekily listed a handful of other conspiracy theories too, and yes, one by one, he nodded – he believed all of them.

It is always interesting to ask people if they can show evidence or proof of their conspiracies, that is not a YouTube video. Or even worse, a Youtube video of someone talking about another Youtube video that they have seen.

Opinions like our own in others are, of course, very attractive, that is how we learn and grow communities. But fixation without an objective viewpoint is never healthy in the long term. I'm not being cynical here, just trying to be honest. Strong beliefs are important, but strong beliefs about anything that are held with only a shred of evidence outside of social media is a dangerous thing. That is how extremism is developed, in dark bedrooms with months of fixation, no external influences or even the cold light of day to shine on dark and dangerous theories.

And even more, fixation combined with the Dunning-Kruger effect just amplifies it all. The Dunning-Kruger effect is simply a wrongly over-inflated sense of our own skill or knowledge on a specific subject, usually because we don't have the self-awareness to realise it, like that guy in the queue.

We all can get very passionate and loud about complex subjects just because we learned a bit about it last night on the news, or we've joined a WhatsApp group with other like-minded people. It is the moment where real experts sigh or grimace politely, like when world leaders hint that we should drink bleach or shine lights into our orifices to cure Covid. Remember that?

Confidence is both good and bad

Confidence is great thing – but over-confidence with limited knowledge can be dangerous. We can easily become ultracrepidarians – yeah I know, my friend David pointed me to this word during lockdown. It may be the longest word that I know, and definitely one I can't pronounce.[13]

An ultracrepidarian is a person who criticises or gives opinions on things beyond their knowledge or expertise. It comes from the Latin phrase ultra crepidam – 'beyond the sole of a shoe' – meaning that a shoemaker should stick to shoemaking.

People will give opinions; some are right, some are wrong, and no matter how loudly they project them, it doesn't change the fact that they are just opinions.

But as I sometimes say after my talks, eat the meat and spit out the bones. That is not bad advice for dealing with people either. Don't eat them, but do bear in mind that their abrasive nature may well be from their insistence on relaying their passionately-held but wrong opinions loudly.

13 It is pronounced uhl-truh-krep-i-dair-ee-uhn

The halo and the horn

The world is a complex place...

People even go into coffee shops now and order a "grande, no-whip, white chocolate, decaf, soy mocha with an extra shot and five pumps of no-sugar syrup[14]".

...so our brain tries to make life a bit simpler for us.

One way it does this is by using what I mentioned above: 'cognitive biases', or shortcuts, if you like. The problem with these, of course, is that they are sometimes wrong and can make us make bad decisions or judge people.

When we meet people, our brain isn't as clean, un-judgmental and perfect as we would like to think it is. We think about and judge people quickly, often within a few seconds.

The long-established 'halo effect' is where we tend to think that more attractive or even taller people are more trustworthy, intelligent and knowledgeable.

And the opposite is the 'horn effect' – where researchers have found that we think that shorter and 'less attractive' people are less trustworthy.

So, we can make quick and unfounded judgments.

This of course is perfectly seen in dating apps where people swipe left or right to reject or shortlist a potential partner. We've all got good and bad photographs of ourselves. I wonder how many people miss out on a good date when they swipe the wrong way, because of a bad photo. A halo or horn photo.

The average height in the UK for a man is 5′9″ (my height) and for a woman it is 5′3″. So, therefore yes, average people are automatically seen as less attractive using this bias.

But it goes even deeper than that.

---

14 This drink is very similar to ones voted the most complex, bizarre and annoying orders ever by baristas on their Reddit thread.

Be careful with first impressions. Just because we might think that more attractive people are more intelligent and trustworthy. It doesn't actually mean that that is true. They just look more attractive and have more symmetrical faces according to research. We can't see inside their brains and we can't grasp their values, morals or integrity by just looking at their chiselled chins and high cheekbones.

So when you see people for the first time, think a bit deeper than your brain bias. When you start a new job, a person you might find annoying on the first day could actually over time become a good friend – or it can work the other way too.

As we go through life, it's important to just pause occasionally to check ourselves and our biases. Be careful not to think that, because Brad Pitt looks attractive and is a good actor, he must also be excellent at algebra or woodwork. Even if our brain tells us that he looks like he'll knock up a cracking coffee table, press pause, look again, enjoy Oceans 11 and go to a proper carpenter for your table.

Our biases can bring us fears too. For example, if you were attacked by a person wearing a black and white striped football top, your brain might tell you to be wary of all Newcastle United supporters in future, even though 99.99% of them are very nice indeed.

Think beyond the 'halo' and the 'horn'. It is good for us and everyone.

A word about difference

The people we meet may well be different to us. Some of these differences are important.

Two key ones are:

- Everyone we meet will have a slightly different personality to us
- Many people we meet will be neurodiverse

Personality types

Personality typing, testing or profiling is a well-worn[15] path with lots of different approaches and names attached. Myers-Briggs and DISC are well known, along with over 2,500 other different tests on the market, with more being launched every year.

As controversial as these are, with claim and counter-claim, they all try to do two things: help us understand ourselves, and help us to interact with others better.

I have done a few of these over the years, but I know the 'Myers-Briggs Type Indicator' (MBTI) best, along with Gallup's 'CliftonStrengths' (formerly 'Strengthsfinder'). These were both explained to me by excellent trainers, who also addressed the downsides and greyer areas of testing. To be honest, they were watershed moments in my life – they stuck, in the right way.

I learned about myself through MBTI, but I really came alive through the use of CliftonStrengths. You can get a basic test for £20 which will show you your top five strengths. When I showed my wife my top five strengths, she said straightaway, "That is you!" Good feedback.

Through that training I also started to understand that I should focus more on my strengths and manage (not major or focus on) my weaknesses. I started to look for opportunities that fitted my strengths, and probably ended up doing what I currently do partly because of the understanding they brought me.

Once you do a few of these tests, it'll help to give you a language to frame yourself in relation to others. It'll help to see your strengths and weaknesses and theirs too, which is gold dust when communicating or being in a team.

---

15 ...and occasionally controversial, as many organisations and researchers fight on the accuracy and market share of their product. Some even say that they are just not true.
https://www.theguardian.com/tv-and-radio/2021/mar/03/they-become-dangerous-tools-the-dark-side-of-personality-tests
https://www.washingtonpost.com/outlook/five-myths/five-myths-about-personality-tests/2018/09/20/3a57a8ee-b78a-11e8-a2c5-3187f427e253_story.html

You'll start to see certain traits too, which is helpful, just don't say it out loud to them or think of these tests as a straitjacket or box. Think of them more of a hint or guide, not a lifelong label.

Neurodiversity

The number of people diagnosed with autistic spectrum disorders has grown 787% since the late 90s. This is due to many factors. More than one in 100 people are on the autistic spectrum – around 700,000 adults and children in the UK, according to the National Autistic Society.

Some autistic people face greater challenges than others as a result of their neurotype. For many, being autistic is a difference rather than a disability and some also view autism as an identity. No two autistic people are the same; the situations that they find difficult vary hugely.

Our view of autism is changing as we learn to understand it better and we learn from people who are neurodivergent.

In day-to-day interactions between autistic and non-autistic people there can be misunderstandings and awkwardness for both parties.

I have a good friend Lynne who is an expert in this area – she encourages everyone to understand it better. She helpfully explains it as a difference in wiring in the brain. People with autism are wired up differently – they see the world differently and communicate with it in a different way. Great communication between autistic and non-autistic people happens when we understand and accept one another's communication differences and are willing to flex our communication style to accommodate others.

It is helpful to bear this in mind when meeting others, as many may not be diagnosed but might show some characteristics of autism.

Lynne coaches individuals and families to communicate more effectively, as she has learnt so much from her son as he grew up and went to University.

It's not a good thing to always generalise, but sometimes it's helpful to understand that people in certain jobs or roles will be, statistically, more likely to be neurodivergent.

Read up on it. Take a course on it. There is a useful concise article in the footnotes.[16]

Learning to let go

People are great, but sometimes they frustrate me, make me perplexed, occasionally hurt me – thankfully, they can amaze me too. We cannot get along with everyone we come across.

When times of conflict or oddness happen, try hard to not take it personally, it probably isn't intended. The other person was just projecting onto you how they feel or believe inside. We've all got stuff we carry around and we all have bad moments or off days. Half of the battle is being kind to ourselves while also developing the self-awareness to help us connect to others in the best way possible.

I have noticed recently that a phrase used a lot is, "I am so over (insert name) now". Unfortunately this is often followed by anger, beef and words that make it very clear that they are clearly not over that person.

Some TV channels make 80% of their programmes based on this situation. It makes addictive brainless slobbing-out-on-the-sofa TV – but long-term ruminating is always bad for us.

Don't say you are 'over' something unless you are. And if you need help, seek it out.

People are complex, and moving on from the bad people experiences we have can be difficult. Sometimes moving on from hurt is instantaneous, sometimes it takes time. Sometimes it needs an hourly or daily reminder to continue to let go. As is written often – don't let anyone live rent-free in your head.

As the Oasis song says, "Don't look back in anger". Or, if you are a Disney fan, then hum that song made famous by the animated film set in a wintry kingdom. For legal reasons I cannot give you the lyrics here, but I

16 https://www.autism.org.uk/advice-and-guidance/what-is-autism

think you may know it: it rhymes with – 'let it snow!'

Find a way, or get help, to look back without all the emotion attached.

I shot the sheriff

When I was an international[17] rapper with my friends, we were travelling to a gig in an A-team style van that someone had lent us. It was one of those vans that had been converted – there was storage space at the back and big comfy bucket seats. It even had a massive carphone on the dashboard, long before most people had mobiles. We were very excited. We were going somewhere in the south, enjoying every bump of the M1 that we got to know so well.

I was driving at the time and everyone in the back of the van got really bored, so they decided that it would be funny to start messing about with a water pistol that they had brought. Unfortunately, the water pistol was a replica of a Glock hand gun. It was around the time of the beginning of gangster rap and my mate Nick thought it would be 'really funny' to fire water at oncoming vehicles as we drove. We were going down a country road, trying to find the field where our festival gig was. As cars came past us, Nick leant out of the window with this replica hand gun and started squirting water at the oncoming traffic.

I had no idea this was happening, but obviously it really freaked out the drivers of oncoming cars. A bit further along I suddenly saw a police car pull in behind us. I thought he was just checking us out, whatever. So I kept going, then another police car pulled in front of us, so we were hemmed in between two top-of-the-range traffic cars. Suddenly, the one in front started to brake hard with his blue lights on, forcing me to slam on the brakes and pull into a lay-by.

We opened the sliding door on the side of the van and the police shouted in a megaphone style, "COME OUT OF THE VAN WITH YOUR HANDS UP!", and "STEP AWAY FROM THE VAN!"

17 Er, well, we did three gigs abroad in all. One of them was on Guernsey, giving us the prestigious honour of being the first ever rap group to perform on the island. There is a blue plaque on that field somewhere, I reckon.

We all got out and the officers went inside the van and picked up, with a pencil, like only policemen did, the offending water pistol which looked like a real gun.

One officer held it up and asked, "Whose is this?" My other mate, Justin, admitted it was his (but it was actually Nick that was doing the shooting). I think the police probably thought it was quite funny. They gave the lads a stern telling-off and allowed us to go back into the van. Thankfully they didn't arrest or shoot us.

I was so embarrassed about this, and worried that the guy who lent us the van would be furious that we kept it quiet. At least until Justin based his whole best man speech around it at my wedding.

Until we got pulled over, I had no idea Nick was 'shooting' oncoming traffic. Why would I even think that? I was oblivious. Some people are aware of their behaviour, they over-think, are introspective and over-analyse every word they say. On the other hand, many people we meet and work with will be just as I was in the van – completely oblivious. They are clueless as to the way they treat others, or make others feel. It's rather like that classic Seinfeld episode, where they meet a guy who is always invading their personal space and speaking to them too closely.

Some people are like a bull in a china shop, some are like little mice tiptoeing through the tulips.

Don't assume that everyone knows how they are being.

Some simply do not. Others definitely do.

People are often unaware of the effect they have on others. If someone hurts us we can think they are thinking about the incident the whole time – even years later. Most of the time they aren't. They are just carrying on and may not have even noticed how they have affected us or others.

So, I am learning to give more people the benefit of the doubt.

A lot of bad things that happen to us are often because of people's cluelessness, rather than their hateful intentions.

The art of waiting

Maybe you've sent an important message to someone, and hours later there's still no reply or acknowledgement. Don't start to catastrophise and think the worse of them. Maybe they just aren't glued to their phone, or they are busy. We have probably all wasted energy waiting for replies to messages, only to get a response 48 hours later from someone who has lost their phone or been out of range.

I am sometimes disappointed, but more often I just needed to wait.

Forgive and remember

I like the concept of forgiveness (possibly seen as old-fashioned these days), and I wonder if we should start to embrace it again. It is very practical, in my experience, and has got me through some tough encounters. It starts to free us up from bad experiences and it also frees the perpetrators from our heads too.

I do believe in justice and law and I don't think people should just be let off and forgiven for everything – that is the comedy sketch version of forgiveness.

The more helpful way to look at forgiveness is this:

> "Forgiving is not forgetting; it's actually remembering – remembering and not using your right to hit back. It's a second chance for a new beginning. And the remembering part is particularly important. Especially if you don't want to repeat what happened." *(Desmond Tutu)*

Forgiveness is also an expression of self-preservation:

- People will hurt us
- It stings
- It can stay with us
- We can ruminate on it
- But then – it takes brain bandwidth to hate people

- It takes vital energy
- It will leak out into our thoughts and actions
- It can make us unhappy
- It can make us untrusting with everyone
- Sometimes it can even make us ill

When people have hurt me, whether intentionally or not. I don't forget, I remember. But the act of one-off, or constant, forgiveness takes the sting out of it. I can start to let go and, over time and with good counsel or a good listening ear, the pain does start to fade away. It eventually gets to the point where I don't go out of my way to meet some people who have hurt me or my loved ones, but if I bumped into them, it would be OK. I'd smile, say hello and carry on with my day.

I got head-butted once playing basketball. This guy faced me up and head-butted me on court after I'd fouled him. It was a bit like one of those dream moments where you wonder, "Did that just really happen to me?" A week later I went to a music gig on my own, and I saw him and his mates walking towards me. I took a deep breath and said hello. We spoke briefly and went on our way. It was a bit awkward, but it was OK. I'm not ever going to be best friends with this guy, but we see each other now and again and we both realise that it was a bad situation. There are no lingering after-effects. Do remember you may not have to see people again; that just happened to me, and thankfully it had a good outcome.

I've been Tango-ed – on the M1!

When I was fairly new to driving - I had a long drive down south in my first car - a very brown 1.1 litre Ford Fiesta 'Popular Plus', I was livin' la vida loca in those days. The big trip was to visit, my then, girlfriend, and I am pleased to say - now wife. Phew. I had packed some snacks, as you do, and I'd got a big new plastic drinks bottle with a built in straw. I loved this bottle and I filled it to the brim with the bright e-number filled fizzy orange juice Tango, and then put the little plastic cap on the big plastic straw.

An hour later I was driving down the M1, it was a sunny day and I was driving at exactly 70 mph, like I am sure you do too. I became thirsty, mainly, for e-numbers, and grabbed my big drinks bottle. I took the little cap of the straw and it exploded everywhere. The drink had been revving up in the car and a fountain of bright orange liquid sugar hit the car roof like a NASA rocket test and covered me in Tango while driving. Somehow I managed to keep the car on the road as the sugary drink dripped off my head and all over my clothes.

I'd put the wrong liquid into the wrong container and I'd sealed it up.

Sometimes I wonder if hard to get on with people are simply under pressure - they are sealed and shaken up in the wrong container. A stressful situation, a job that doesn't suit them or when they are totally out of their comfort zone. Feeling lost at sea and under resourced. Wedding speeches are a great example of this. People say the bizarrest and often most inappropriate things. I have seen some howlers over the years, often fuelled by people feeling cooped up, out of their depth and lubricated by three pints of the wedding speech embarrassment maker.

When people are under pressure they can say stuff they wouldn't normally say and do stuff they wouldn't normally do. They may even hurt us and others in the process.

Most of the time in these situations, it's best to pause, recognise the stressful context, the pressured situation - shrug and laugh it off.

I have mentioned shrugging a few times now, it is underrated in these odd situations, along with a notebook to write it down.

Angry people are often just under pressure, like we all get from time to time. We used to get our Christmas turkey from our local butchers, trying to do the right thing buying local, knowing it would be fresh. One year we went to order it and the co-owner was so stressed out. She was hating every moment of being there and when we mentioned turkeys she got all tense and a feeling of dread seemed to come over her. Bless her, we were trying to do the right thing, as well as helping to grow her business, but she made it such an ordeal. We made our order and tip toed out of the shop. She made a pre-Christmas task really stressful. The next year, they didn't do turkeys at all. They decided to stop doing them. A butchers who refused to sell meat. If they had employed someone temporarily it would have been fine. Wrong person, wrong place, wrong time, under pressure.

Everyone is carrying a load and has a backstory we know nothing about - there is always history and hurt. And yes I do agree that hurt people hurt people.

History and hurt

I keep this at the back of my mind these days when awkward people come across my path. It has been proven to be true so many times.

We have no idea of the battle that someone is fighting or the history and hurt they have.

Like a child who is really scared of dogs. Either they have been attacked by a dog, or been told by others that dogs are dangerous. They become permanently scared of them. The same can happen with wasps. For most people a wasp sting is slightly painful but not life-threatening (unless they are severely allergic) but some people act as if a wasp will sever their arm if it came near them. Most of the time a wasp will not bother us. I don't like them, they get on my nerves but I try not to panic. For many it's a genuine phobia, learnt behaviour from others or their own history of getting stung or seeing someone stung.

We were on a dolphin-watching boat trip in Ireland when our kids were little. We were sat in rows on the bench seats facing each other until we got to the dolphin watching area. Twenty minutes into the trip an adult sitting opposite my daughter panicked when a wasp came near their sandwich and batted the wasp away, sending it angrily straight into my daughters face and it stung her. We were on the sea, I am not even sure how it got there to be honest. The wasp that is - not the adult. Without the history and hurt of the wasp-batting adult, my daughter would not have got stung. Their reaction hurt my daughter.

Stress factor

I worked with a client once, they were part of large public organisation who obviously booked speakers every year for staff events. My first interaction with them felt a little odd, I couldn't put my finger on it and I should have walked away at that point, but I didn't, and to be honest it was in the early days of my work and I needed the gig.

As the event came closer their behaviour became more and more controlling and paranoid. They wanted to know everything I was going to say and they checked a few times about my invoicing procedures and the full amount of the mileage I was going to charge. They also wanted to do everything on email too and did not like speaking on the phone, never a good sign in my experience. Email is great to confirm things, but terrible for discussing things.

When I got to the hotel to speak, I could feel the tension with the organiser. The talk itself went pretty well; the delegates were a little quiet at first but I got them warmed up in the end, phew.

Reflecting on this person's behaviour after the event, I mentioned it to a speaker friend of mine and he knew exactly who it was. He had had a bad experience with them too. I guess I should have asked him. My learning from that event many years later is that they probably had some history with a bad speaker (not my friend!), maybe they were ripped off by them or got a big expenses bill they weren't expecting. Maybe they had someone who didn't deliver what they had promised either. That – along with a tight budget, a strict billing department, and possibly an over-controlling boss – probably turned the organiser into a worried and mistrusting micro-manager.

The history and hurt this person had with other speakers and some of their colleagues made the whole thing feel like I was wading through treacle. Ironic for a motivational event. I did my best that day, I made the most of it despite the treacle-wading, but I won't be working with them again and I won't refer anyone else to them either. I had tried to encourage them to trust me more for both the billing (which is never a surprise, as I spell it out beforehand) and the content on the day, but their history and hurt was so engrained they just couldn't let go. The tension was palpable. It must be such a stressful place to work.

A simple way to have a happier workplace

People are often looking for lots of complex ways to have a better work experience, they spend a fortune on courses and books, they listen to dozens of podcasts and gurus. But sometimes to have a happier workplace, the simple things can really work.

Have you ever had a day when people really annoy you at work? I have. In fact, sometimes, I secretly thought, "What is wrong with these people!" If we are irritable, or in the wrong frame of mind, we can easily be distracted by people and get annoyed at every little thing they do. That's life, and work I guess.

So you might be in a barracks, sharing an office or on an online training session together and people might start to say ridiculous things or just do something annoying. Unless something serious is happening, the best advice is to bite your lip, and choose your battles wisely.

We can't fight everything and everyone. We can't correct every crazy opinion we hear. We can't spend our life and work trying to relentlessly change people's opinions or habits. 99.9% of the time the only person we can truly change is ourselves.

So, we DON'T have to react, we can choose to bite our lip, take a deep breath, say nothing, or just walk away. We don't have to get involved in an argument or a piece of gossip. That's a choice we make.

I'm not saying we shouldn't have an opinion at all or that we should be silent about everything. It's about choosing our battles carefully.

We can't fight everyone at work, in life or – especially – online! I choose my battles much more now. I choose to say nothing and walk away more now – yes, even extroverts like me can do it.

After all - we are all annoying sometimes too.

To have a less stressful time at work, choose…

…to say a bit less

…to smile a bit more

…to roll your eyes secretly

…to listen more

…your work friends very carefully

…to keep your head down

…to get your job done with a lot less drama

Don't contort yourself to fit in

The author Brené Brown has done so much great work on human behaviour - authenticity, relationships and belonging.

She helped me understand that the opposite of belonging is not loneliness, it is trying to fit in. True belonging is being accepted for you, but trying to fit in is often changing who you are to be accepted for being like everyone else.

The difference is life-changing.

Without a doubt there's been moments in my life, both when I was younger and getting older, when I have tried to fit in, where I've tried to be part of a group – and eventually realised that group simply wasn't for me.

When I first started writing books, I got some advice from a bestselling author. He told me that I should never write a book in a way that wasn't truly me, that I should always use my authentic voice. In my case that meant – even if it is not perfect grammar or perfect prose – it was important for me to find my own voice. That is literal sometimes for me, as some of my books are wholly or partially dictated first, then edited, rather than being written from a blank screen and the keyboard. It is my voice you hear.

I remember when I was transitioning from my old job running a charity into my new role as a speaker, the first couple of years were pretty stressful. I was so keen to learn from others that I took on board almost everything that was said when I was meeting with other speakers. I wore myself out trying to be like everybody else and do things like everyone else when I just wasn't ready. And the revelation came when I realised that people booked me to solve a problem, sure, but also they booked me because of who I am, because of a video they'd seen, or an article that they had read.

I'm not everyone's cup of tea, nobody is, but I think I find the clients that I work with best, and I'm also happy to let other clients go.

Colleagues have been surprised that I have deliberately walked away from potential earnings because I realise my values didn't match, and I wasn't going to jump through their hoops in order to fit in. I don't think that's arrogance – it's just me knowing who I am and who will I work with best.

Some people can spend their whole lives trying to fit in, not finding a true family, community or tribe. I'm glad that I have found a few communities that I can belong to.

...Where do you feel you truly belong without becoming someone else?

...Have you found that place or people group yet?

...Have you ever been in a group, but have not been fully accepted and valued?

Practical task

Today - choose deliberately to see the good in everyone you meet. Even if you can't stretch to that at times - choose to see their potential.

Try it. Then reflect: How did it affect you, your day, or your mood?

QUICK WINS

Arguments

People with the weakest arguments, sometimes shout the loudest. They find social media particularly helpful, as it creates the illusion that their weak argument is true as other people will agree with them too. Thats how numbers work, there will always be someone to agree with every weak argument or crazy idea that we have.

It can be a dangerous game.

Saying sorry

Sorry is a strong word these days, not spoken as often in public as it was. It's often danced around by celebrities and organisations trying to tiptoe through the PR and legal minefields they find themselves in.

But when said with real feeling and without excuses, saying sorry is very powerful to heal relationships. We all get things wrong, and sometimes we just need to say it. If you are a parent, it is important for your kids to see and hear you say it too.

A world where people either pretend to be perfect or never say sorry is a recipe for ongoing disconnection.

We have to be careful though. In personal relationships, just say sorry once – don't spend your life apologising for things that happened years ago. One sincere apology is enough, then look forward and keep on going.

Homophily: we tend to flock together

Sometimes I wonder whether we simply don't get on with other people or we find ourselves disconnected with other people because we are just different to them. Homophily means that we tend to be attracted to people who are similar to us.

I have friends from different countries, different backgrounds and different races but most of my close friends probably sound like and may even look a little bit like me. Poor things. One of my friends particularly is probably my double, although I feel that I am the more attractive one, of course. He disagrees, naturally.

It's obvious that we will flock together with others that have similar interests, views, values and beliefs – it is more comfortable that way. Most of my close friends have vaguely similar political views as me, not all of them, but most. It makes sense, I don't want to spend my down time arguing with people or having to persuade people of my views, it is exhausting. For a good night out, or a good night in watching a film, I want to hang out with people who understand me and accept me, and they will feel the same.

Worldviews

Everyone has a worldview.

Their worldview is key, but it is often invisible to them, like it is with us. It is the lens we look through. A lens coloured by our background, upbringing, culture, values and beliefs.

It is important to our understanding of ourselves but also to why some people might not get on with us or display behaviour that we just don't understand. There's no right or wrong here, it is what it is, we are all just different.

Even though it can bring moments of confusion and conflict, the world is a better place for it. One worldview would be so dull.

Big family and work get-togethers

Families and workplaces are groups of people thrown together with little choice in the matter.

Family gatherings – Christmas, birthdays or holidays – can be difficult. With possibly only a gene pool or relation by marriage in common, a group of people are cooped up together for several days or longer, with all those personalities, opinions, views, ages and beliefs simmering away and clashing.

We don't choose our family and usually we don't choose our workmates, unless you're the boss of course, but – trust me – employing people just like you is a nightmare. A team needs to be made up of different skills and different views, but with one shared purpose. People who work together are often just people who share the same carpet or email address domain during the week. Some workmates become partners or good friends, some we never see again. That is why workplace parties can be so awkward: what we have in common is sometimes only work.

In conclusion

After reading all the advice, experience and research here - we ultimately have three healthy options when a disconnect happens and our relationships are challenging or get damaged.

We can:

- **Repair**
- **Retune**
- **Release**

Repair is always the most awkward one.

We can hold our hands up and say sorry, we can try to build a bridge if we messed up. Or if they messed up we can be assertive, kind and try to repair things. It does, of course, bring the risk of rejection or maybe, even worse, ambivalence. Sometimes repairing works, sometimes it doesn't, but it is often worth a go. It is usually best done in private, by the way – never in front of others.

Retune is a lot less risky, but takes a bit of practice for new habits to be formed.

For example, you had a good friend who has become a bit more distant over the last year or so. Their life has changed, they have got kids now and they live a bit further away than they did. At this point the connection may be cooling off a little so you retune the dial from "we are really close" to "we are not as close as we were". You put them on a different list or they move away from the centre of your life a little.

It may be sad, but no relationships last forever; people come and go as life changes. You can use the analogy of a train station, with people coming and going, trains leaving and arriving all the time.

Another example: think of being in school and your mate from the last school year is not quite as keen now. You realise that you do all the running in the relationship, they always want you to go to their house, they never come to yours anymore and often they cancel arrangements at the last minute. I'd retune that person from good friend to school day acquaintance. Turn the dial, tweak and retune the connection.

And with that, change your boundaries and expectations of them and the relationship. It would be nice to hear from them occasionally, but you know you're not going to organise your weekend around them, as they may let you down.

Invest and cultivate better friendships.

Release is the final step. The biggest step for us; they may never know about it.

In my experience, people either want to get rid of people too early, because repairing is hard, or they hang on to people too long. If someone continues to hurt you, is abusive to you, has made it clear they don't want to stay connected to you, or just for your own sanity – release them.

We are not designed to stay connected with everyone we meet. Some encounters are just fleeting, some people we don't gel with, some are horrible to deal with, want us to be something else or, as I have mentioned, just want us for what they can get out of us. These are the people that we remember, but forgive and release in our heads – once, or maybe many times.

These are the people whose memory we want to fade away as our life is better without them. They were exhausting. They took up too much brain space. Some we may release for a time and they come back as better people, some we release back in to the wild forever. Even a growing plant needs pruning from time to time.

No one should be allowed to steal your joy, not for more than a few minutes anyway.

> People often say that motivation doesn't last. Well, neither does bathing – that's why we recommend it daily.
>
> ***Zig Ziglar***

3

How to get motivated

DEEP DIVE

Back to basics

Feeling stuck?

Got something big to do but keep putting it off?

Want to make the first steps to a goal?

This back to basics chapter is for you. It's about getting something done, and understanding the process. When reading this section of the book, it is best to think of any big task, challenge or deadline that you have as you read.

I'm going to split this first section into three parts:

1. **Get Real**
2. **Get Ready**
3. **Get Results**

So, let's just press pause on your life now, and find out where you're at.

1. GET REAL

Where are you right now?

The basics of getting the best out of ourselves is pressing pause and asking the big question. Where am I right now?

If you've ever used the maps or a satnav on your phone, you'll know that it does three things:

1. It finds out where you are
2. It asks you where you want to go
3. It prepares the best route for you

But it can't do anything until it finds out where you are - my phone sometimes freezes at this point and I get stuck, but once the phone has that information only then can it plan ahead and find the best route.

So, where are you? Be honest, I know its not very easy, but it's important.

The following questions are used in various forms and are a great tool to take stock of life. Don't be tempted to skip this. On the next page is my version of the 'wheel of life' that I've used in hundreds of sessions over the years:

Simply give yourself an honest score from 1 to 10, where 10 is perfect and 1 is very bad, but don't write a number in the segments – shade it in with a pencil, so you can see where the wheel is balanced and where it needs some work. A wobbly wheel can show we don't have much balance in our life. We could be working hard, earning loads but have no fun and no rest; that can make the wheel, and us a bit wobbly.

This simple tool is something you can come back to and use as a way of checking on your life and your progress and where you need to get more balance. For example, during the Covid lockdown I am pretty sure that our wheels were very unbalanced. Some would have had a sourdough section, some learning a foreign language, and some wearing pyjamas for a Zoom meeting in the wheel too.

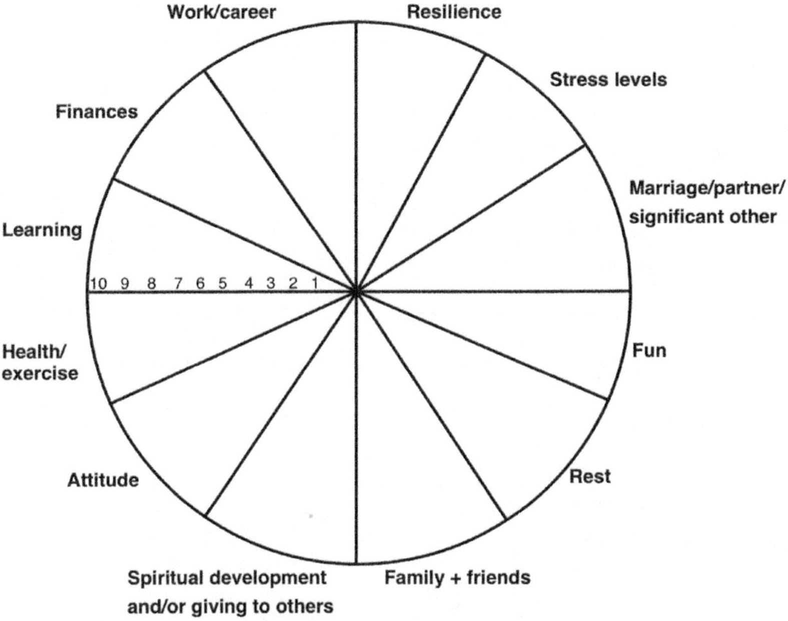

It is just good to check from time to time. A check-up-from-the-neck-up as they say.

Ok, great. If you've done that then we know where you are. Now we can start to look forward.

Beliefs

Our beliefs are very powerful. They change the way we feel and the way we look and interact with the world around us.

Our mind works a bit like this:

HISTORY—>THOUGHTS —> BELIEFS —> FEELINGS —> ACTIONS

Our history can become our thoughts. our thoughts can become our beliefs, our beliefs affect the way we feel, and our feelings affect our actions.

Back in the 90s there was a report of a man called Sam Shoeman[18] who was diagnosed with cancer and was given only months to live. He died as expected in the timescale they gave him, but at the autopsy it transpired that the doctors had got it wrong. Sam's cancer was very small, and hadn't even spread. So, according to one doctor, the man died of believing he had terminal cancer, not from actually having terminal cancer.

Our beliefs change the way we see the world and how we interact with it. Misguided beliefs can knock us out of shape.

You might have seen the story of the turtle called Peanut.

(Photo used with the kind permission of the Missouri Department of Conservation)

Peanut got the plastic holder from a six-pack of beer caught over her shell, and because she wasn't able to remove it she had it on for four years as she grew. She has become the poster turtle to encourage people not to leave litter.

Eventually Peanut was found and freed from the little plastic prison, but this piece of plastic had distorted her shell so much that she didn't grow and develop fully. A tiny thing changed her life. False beliefs are much the same: they seem tiny, but can affect us.

18 https://pubmed.ncbi.nlm.nih.gov/1546347/

You have so much potential, so don't let wrong ideas and beliefs take hold and affect your future. Life is way too precious for that.

Become realistically positive

I've met people who believe that they are superior to others. This is never good, arrogance is a horrible trait that only leads to having no friends, being lonely and eventually, a rude awakening. You only have had to see the aggressive people on the early rounds of music audition reality shows to see that. They were the ones that shouted and screamed that they didn't get through, and they often say or do something rude, storm off or get bundled out by security. Not a good look.

Just as bad as arrogance is the other side of the coin, where we think very little of ourselves, feeling like everyone is out to get us and we are worthless.

This can lead to all sorts of problems.

Our beliefs about ourselves seriously affect our lives.

I think there is a great way to get our beliefs and attitude right. It's called many things I'm sure, but I like to call it being 'realistically positive'. It's doing what you've just done - finding out where you are, believing the real truth about your potential and then having real hope and being positive for the future - while not ignoring the challenges we face.[19]

Blind and aggressive positive thinking has been proven to be toxic and can make us ignore very real things in our lives, like illness for instance. Being realistically positive is a good attitude to have, it is about hope in the face of challenges, and planning to get around them, not blind positivity, ignoring life's real obstacles. There is a subtle, but very important difference there.

---

19 In his book *Good to Great*. author Jim Collins refers to this and formed his concept of the 'Stockdale Paradox', around the prisoner-of-war story from Admiral Jim Stockdale, that the people to lose hope quickest are surprisingly the optimists. More info here: https://www.jimcollins.com/concepts/Stockdale-Concept.html

So here's the deal - people like you and me have good times and not-so-good times, we have good days and not-so-good days. That's called life.

But what we can do is learn to be more hopeful and positive than negative. The world bombards negativity at us and people do too. The trick is to be tough enough on the outside to keep on going while still being soft enough in the middle to enjoy life, family and friends.

Whenever we are aiming for something, between now and the destination there will be challenges, but after a bit of a sulk we need to find a way out of that, because a new-day attitude starts when you decides it does. In fact sleep is like switching our laptop off and on again. We can draw a line and start afresh anytime we want.

So find out what gets your head in a more positive place and use that often. It might be some of the advice from this book, getting outside, playing sport, chatting to friends, having a night out or a quiet night in – whatever it is, use those things to retain balance and stay positive. I can guarantee you this – a realistically positive outlook will always get you a better result. That is a big truth, that I've learned the hard way. Hopeful, positive and determined, yet relaxed, is a great way to be. Find ways to maintain that or get yourself back to that better place. You, but on a good day, as they say.

If you're reading this book one day before a big event like a final exam it won't make that much difference, but if you are reading this a few weeks, months or even two years before an event or exam, it could make a big difference. That's being realistically positive. We can do life well and achieve, but contrary to what social media ads say, things take time - more on that shortly.

Our fundamental beliefs about ourself

So, what should we believe about ourselves? Well, as my friend and creator of the famous blob tree tool, Pip Wilson, says, "You are beautiful" – you are a beautiful human being (whether you feel like it or not).

- Not a human doing – we don't have to do amazing things to have worth.
- Not a human buying – we don't have to have expensive stuff to be worth something.
- Just a human being – we just have to 'be'.

And the biggest trick of all is to not let circumstances or others take that away from us.

That's because (and just in case you don't know, or have forgotten) you are a unique person; there's no-one quite like you and there will never be anyone quite like you. You are on this earth for a reason and a purpose. And a big part of that purpose might just be at the other side of your challenge. You might want to be a great presenter, lawyer, or engineer, a great midwife, coder or teacher. That stuff will involve more challenging times and aiming for the best results you are capable of.

We can't travel back in time. But we can change our future. Starting now.

It is simple, but it won't be easy.

Because simple isn't the same as easy.

That's where hard work comes in. Something most of us don't like, but we know deep down it is needed. A few small changes can add up to a better brighter future.

2. GET READY

Commitment

In my days working in lots of schools in the 90's I worked in an inner city school in Leeds which was, according to the government league tables, the second worst school in the country. I loved it there.

I worked there every Friday and sometimes on other days too, doing lessons, lunchtime clubs, sports teams, a bit of mentoring, and assemblies.

Someone who sat in my assemblies a few times was Nicola. She lived nearby and went to that school. Nicola's Mum, Dee, was a single parent. One day Nicola's Mum wanted to go to her aerobics class, but her childminder cancelled, so she took Nicola and her brother Kurtis to the gym with her. At the time there was a children's boxing class happening so Nicola joined in. The rest, as they say, is history.

Nicola Adams was the first ever woman boxer to win an Olympic gold, in London in 2012. She defended her Olympic title in Rio in 2016, went professional in 2017, and was undefeated until her retirement on medical grounds in 2019 with five wins professionally. She literally is the face of women's boxing. An amazing achievement.

After 2012, a few speakers like myself in the Professional Speaking Association (aka the PSA) reached out to medal-winning Olympians to offer free help with their speaking skills as they were launched into the speaking circuit. I approached Nicola and asked her manager if she would like any help with prepping a post Olympic talk. I had several emails from her team and we met in a hotel in Leeds, and then we arranged to meet a few weeks afterwards.

I went down to the GB Boxing training gym in Sheffield to meet her. I got there a bit early, signed in and waited for Nicola to finish her session. I saw her in the gym, pounding away at this water bag. She was really going for it. She finished, took a sip of water, and came in to see me in the meeting room where I helped her to map out her story a bit, so she would be able to use that when she's speaking.

But the first thing I noticed was that she wasn't really out of breath! After pounding away at that bag I would have been a sweaty mess. She walked in the room, hardly breaking a sweat. Her fitness level was unbelievable. She was lovely to be with too, , very keen, really chatty. I never saw her when I was at school. As a youth worker and the guy that did assemblies, I probably bumped into her at some point but she was just a teenager on a corridor I guess in those days. But it was great to catch up and realise that she's from the city that I love and became such an amazing boxer.

I'd like to think that my work in that school had a massive impact on Nicola's life, but that is just not true, she didn't even recognise me. Which I think was helpful for my ego, I was part of a team in school and we all played our part in these teenagers' lives. She didn't need my help – she knew from the age of 13 that she wanted to be Olympic champion. At the time women were not even allowed to compete in boxing, due to some 100-year-old archaic rule that premenstrual syndrome made women 'too unstable to box' (insert rolling eyes emoji here!). But she fought and trained hard. Her first match was in a smoke-filled local working men's club, but she achieved her dream in 2012, on home soil. In Leeds city centre she even has a gold-painted postbox, a high honour indeed.

Hard work

When you look at the way that someone excels in a sport it is a bit boring to be honest, because it's just hard work. Nicola would have had to work on her defensive and offensive moves. She had to work on her fitness levels and, and she told me, she had to look at all of her opponents in depth. When I met her she was in her 30s and I asked her, how do you beat the younger, faster boxers? She said, "I use my experience more now, I can dodge more punches and let them wear themselves out a little bit and then attack them and win that way". Clever stuff. As we get older, we change the way we play sport and we use some of our experience.

So let's be honest, on one level, there's nothing special about Nicola Adams – she was just a kid from an inner-city neighbourhood in Leeds who accidentally found out that she liked boxing and then put in the work. Mentally and physically. It's amazing how we sometimes idolise people who've literally just learned how to work hard. Nicola got better every time, better after every bout and just kept working. Her pinnacle, of course, was the 2012 Olympics where she became a household name, appeared on every talk show and became a role model for many.

So maybe you have a big dream or goal – something outrageous. What if we could do the same and achieve like Adams? Well, like Nicola, we have to commit to a journey that we're on. We have to make the changes to get further. And that word 'commit' is often the stumbling block.

Commitment takes, er, commitment.

It's simply about understanding what we need to do in order to get the best out of ourselves. It is not exciting. But it is important.

I'm sure Nicola didn't get up every morning with a smile on her face, leaping out of bed and dancing towards the boxing gym. I'm sure there were times when she wanted to blob out and eat three deep pan pizzas. She'll have had bad days just like us. But she knew that commitment pays, and she saw it proven that when she does what she needs to do she simply got results. And we can too, once we know what we need to do, we can use the greatest gift we ever have to make change really happened.

Time

Time works. It's always there, it can't be stopped, but it can be used for good. If we flick the switch.

Flick the switch from wasting time, ignoring time and just hoping it will help us somehow without putting in the effort, or changing anything.

We can flick the switch now. Flick it to, "I know where I'm at, so I now know what I need to do". Once we know what you need to do to make a difference, we can use time well. It becomes our friend, not our enemy.

We start with deciding, an intent on our part. We have to commit. We decide and chip away until we get good. We start to make it happen and then see what happens.

Will you achieve more straightaway with commitment and intent? Hopefully. But if not, keep on going and watch your results get better and better as time passes.

Going back to Nicola Adams – she couldn't become a better boxer overnight, but with the right work put in she became better every day: bit by bit, punch by punch.

Time passed and then she checked again in three months time, and she was much better than she used to be.

Athletes often do this in the 'off-season' where they take one part of their sport and work for three or four months just on that. Then, when the season starts again, they have a new weapon. Simple. They use time well, and we can too. Sometimes we can turn things around overnight, but that is rare, but I can tell you that time will make things happen if you put in the effort too.

To really make it happen, we have to take responsibility for our actions though and commit to changing our sometimes not-so-good habits. Otherwise nothing will happen.

Wishy washy

Wishing something will change has never helped anyone, but doing something different and for the better has always delivered results.

This is often the sticking point though. People often don't take responsibility for their life and their actions.

I've seen it to the level where people think that someone else is in control and life sort of happens to them or they spend their life with their fingers in their ears shouting, "Lalalalalalalalalala".

No matter what your age, you are the driver of your bus. Don't be a passenger.

Get your team sorted

I know we are talking about individual success here, but I still think we need a team to get us there. Everyone has a team, even if they don't know it. Nicola had coaches and trainers helping her, she even explained to me the meals that got delivered to the gym. Normal meals, but with the unhealthy stuff taken out.

I sometimes speak about the BBC show *The Apprentice*. You know the one, where a load of wannabe business people, who've just bought a new suit and think they can be Lord Sugar's next big thing, make a fool of themselves? It's an entertaining show at times, but it stops there for me. It's not about business, its about entertainment. Business just isn't like that. I know people who've been on the show and they told me how it's filmed: non-stop, relentless and edited to make it seem more exciting than it is most of the time. Especially the funny things they say in the boardroom, which is filmed over several hours, not just ten minutes like we see. I hate the way they always seem to lie, cheat and have a go at each other.

Fundamentally what the show forgets to say is that it takes a team to build a business. It takes a team to get you through life too. We'll unpack this more later on.

A bit of history

When Roman soldiers went into battle they would often lock their shields together. These shields had special edges on them so they could be locked together easily. They knew that they would be stronger together rather than on their own. Imagine 100 soldiers tiptoeing around on their own in their sandals, or 100 soldiers with shields clicked together advancing on the army like a big metal tortoise. I know where I'd rather be when the arrows and rocks are flying around me! I'd rather be in a team advancing – than on my own, vulnerable, in danger and in sandals!

Now, don't get me wrong – most of what we need to do is in our own heads, but a good team – family, community, friends, whatever you call them – will help us get there easier.

Get your toolkit ready

I remember revising for my big school exams aged 16, and for some reason I was using this really cheap tiny pen that I think I got off my Grandad. I think he'd taken it from the local betting shop. It was rubbish and just didn't flow at all, so I wasted loads of time trying to get it to work. Not very helpful with exams just around the corner, so my Mam bought me a new pen. We need to get the right tools.

When I'm getting ready to go out to speak I always take at least two bags/cases with me, one with my props and notes in and the other with my laptop and techie stuff. Then I put those bags near my front door so I can't go out without falling over them. It's so much better than panicking in the morning. Get your toolkit together and get a toolbox/bag/case. Simple things like that can help. If you were a plumber you'd have all your stuff ready. It needs planning the night before, so we can be ready for action the next day.

Get your toolkit ready – but be careful, don't use getting your toolkit sorted as an excuse not to do some work. Procrastination often ends up in online shopping and over planning instead of cracking on with what we need to do: in my case right now – writing this book. The amount of things that have stopped me writing this book is staggering. So get your stuff ready. Don't spend four hours searching for the best pencil to buy. Just buy a half decent pencil[20] and get on with it.

3. GET RESULTS

Now, hopefully, you know where you are, and you've got your stuff more ready – it is now time to see yourself through to the results you deserve. The end of your goal may be months, if not, years away. So how do we keep pushing on until that time?

There is another section on this later in the book - but here are a few tips:

"Often when a challenge comes our way the natural response is to stop moving, to give up and not 'step out'. This is the easier choice for it demands very little from us. For our talent to grow we must keep stepping through the rough times to reach the desired goal. There is no other way and no shortcut. To avoid the test is to miss out on part of life's great tapestry, it is part of the course set before us. The development of our ability to endure is key in times of challenge and change…"

(Taken from the book *Keep Stepping* by the late, great, Joy Marsden, used with the kind permission of her family.)

> Even if you're on the right track, you'll get run over if you just sit there.
>
> ***Will Rogers***

20 My preference being the yellow and black Staedtler ones, by the way, because yes, I have spent too much time researching it so you do not have to.

Keep on moving

The key, as the 80's band Soul II Soul said, is to keep on moving. Keep plugging away, because when we are moving we are being active and our brain is more engaged. If we spend ages doing nothing towards our aim, it obviously slows our progress down but also can get us into ingrained bad habits.

We all have times where we need to rest of course, but we also need to learn to keep active. I mean that literally too – do some activity, go to the gym, take a walk, play netball or football. Keeping moving helps our bodies and our brains to stay healthy. I don't feel so good when I haven't exercised for a few days, it's part of life's natural rhythm: move and rest, work and rest, work and run even. In fact, even when you are plugging away, it's best to have a rest and change your scene anyway, so do an hour then get a drink or run up and down your street. Anything to keep your brain active.

My grandparents' generation would often say, "A change is as good as a rest". In this case they may be right. After finishing this paragraph I just got up and made a cup of tea, and now I'm back, ready for the next bit. I know this isn't very exciting; I could have said that I finished this section and then flew my helicopter to Scunthorpe. Sadly, I don't have a helicopter and I don't know anyone in Scunthorpe.

Put (the right stuff) in (to) the hours

Don't just put in time, that is a given, as we have talked about using time well. But even more important is what you put into the hours you do work. It's so easy to get distracted by Youtube, socials, the radio or the TV when we are pushing on. Even researching stuff can sometimes be distracting when we click on an advert and drift to our socials and start doom scrolling. We need to put the right stuff and right effort into the hours we do have.

Get your stuff ready, switch off your distractions, and then be tough enough with yourself to just keep on working without distractions.

Working well means doing it uninterrupted. The easiest way is by finding that special button on your phone; that magical button – you know the one – that turns your phone off.

If you are constantly interrupted, especially on knowledge-based, brain-heavy tasks, the information just doesn't go into our brains so well and it can take us ages to get back into the flow – twenty minutes in one study. Switch your phone and your distractions off, get your work done and then switch it all back on again.

Simple. But, yes, you've guessed it – not easy.

If we switch our phone off to be less distracted on our key tasks, there are two things I can promise you will happen…

1. You'll get better and deeper work done without distractions
2. You will still have friends at the end of the hour

Unless we are a doctor on emergency call, we must find ways in the week to be uncontactable and undisturbed. Let us not over-inflate our importance in the big scheme of things, thinking that the world cannot run without us being connected 24/7. We are supposed to be undistracted occasionally. Being 'on' and available 24 hours a day is one of the things that makes us all more stressed and less productive. We need more honesty and cultural change in this area.

Go for it. Put the right stuff into the hours, don't let them drift.

Twenty minutes of focus is far better than two hours of distractions or displacement activities like scrolling TikTok or wondering if we should put our fridge's contents into alphabetical order. That is nice, but it won't help you achieve your potential, unless of course you are a paid professional procrastinator.

Make things happen, don't just get things done

It's easy to get stuff done. To tick little things off a list, easy stuff, but the key is to make the important things happen too. Do the big stuff first. Trust me – that alone will change your life.

If we are honest we may have a to-do list in your head, it might look a bit like this…

1. Tidy the house
2. Find out about the latest Netflix shows
3. Post a selfie/meme
4. Listen to that new band you've heard about
5. Get your bag ready for work
6. Prep for that big interview coming up
7. Put your pens into alphabetic order of colour
8. Like all the posts on your friends social media
9. Try that new ice cream flavour you just read about

If we just want to get things done then we'll do 1, 2, 3, 4, 7, 8 and 9. We'll be busy and feel like we've done stuff. But 5 is pretty important, and 6 is the biggie. Author Brian Tracy quoted Mark Twain and famously called it 'Eat That Frog'.

We have to learn to do the big stuff first and do the other stuff when we have finished or when we are on a break from the big stuff, or, dare I say it, maybe even not at all.

Don't be busy just working hard, work smart. Do the big ugly frog-shaped stuff first, the other stuff will take care of itself. The key is to do what we need to do, because there is never enough time to do everything we could do. As I will continue to remind people, we cannot complete Netflix or Amazon.

> The things that matter most must never be at the mercy of the things that matter least.
>
> ***Johann Wolfgang von Goethe***

Finish well!

Finishing well means keeping on going until the job is done. It's about taking action, the right action that you know is right - deep down. Life is better and more fun when we take responsibility for our actions, pursue our learning and life goals with a real purpose and passion. 'The rush' of crossing the finish line is great to experience.

Imagine, now, you achieving what you've worked hard for. Grabbing that feeling can help us to move forward.

Life is not an infinite game with no end, that is exhausting, think of it as a series of tasks, challenges, joys and experiences to face, learn from and to achieve.

Here's a simple way to make those those tasks more do-able…

10 point plan for simple effective action – tell it to yourself, now and often...

10. I won't wait for my peers - I'll take the first step.

9. It's down to me.

8. I'm going to start now.

7. I'll give it my best shot.

6. I will not blame someone else.

5. Just watch me!

4. It's the reason I'm on earth after all.'

3. As Nike says – Just Do It!

2. 'I will', not 'I might' but 'I will'.

1. I know that it's Me. Not them, but Me that'll make it happen (I will do this).

Create a strong positive intent, not for everything, but for tasks and challenges. One of my friends who coaches fellow women in business, tells me she uses the phrase, "It is time to put your big girl pants on" – not a phrase I would use (and not a phrase restricted to women), but I think I know what she means.

Don't talk, just act. Don't say, just show. Don't promise, just prove.

Find your way to finish a task strong.

My quick, effective action plan:

Starting today I know deep down that I need to:

1. **Do more…**

2. **Do less…**

3. **Prioritise…**

4. **Talk to…**

5. **Get help with…**

I will do the above (because I know it is best for me and it will help me grow)

Signed: ....

Dated: ....

(Well done, now treat yourself to something nice!)

DEEP DIVE

Why and how

Here is a secret about the personal development industry.

They might dress it up as something different, but motivational speakers like myself only really ever talk about three things (don't tell them I'm telling you this.)

It's the 'why'. Why do we do stuff. It's the how, how do we practically do stuff, and it's the resilience bit, or the 'keeping on going' as I call it. I've done a lot of writing, speaking and videos around these things. So when we think of a big task or even a huge secret goal, we need to think…

Why am I doing this?

How do I do this?

and

How do I keep on going?

That's really the foundation of what personal motivation is, once we know the big why, and then we learn the skills, the how, and then we can start to learn how to be more resilient and to keep on going when we fail.

Why?

So let's look at the 'why'. For example, why do I work here?

We've all had days like that at work. I had a lot more until I became my own boss, for sure, but even then the downside of running your own business eventually kicks in: the realisation that the buck stops with me. Awkward, at first.

I visit loads of different workplaces in my work. I might be in a school one day, and then in the NHS, and then a firm of solicitors. That is one of the reasons I love what I do. No week is the same. In all the time I've spent in other people's workplaces as a visiting speaker, I've realised that most people spend their time at work just getting on with it and are often so busy that they rarely take time out to stop and think why they do what they do.

It is a privilege to be someone who gets them to stop and think why they work there, why they keep coming back and how they can enjoy work more.

"That's all very nice Lee, but they work for the money."

Yes, as Zig Ziglar once said: "Money isn't the most important thing in life, but it's reasonably close to oxygen on the 'gotta have it' scale".

When you look at research into money and motivation at work, you'd be surprised.

Money only motivates people for a very short time. A pay rise often only motivates people for a couple of weeks and then that's it. Some even say that it is the thought of the money alone that is the real motivator, not even the money in the bank. We easily forget it, especially if it goes straight into our bank account, and we then, on a daily basis, often become more bothered about working hours, conditions, the leadership style and who is buying the milk this week.

So if work isn't just about money for many, what is it that keeps us there?

Well, it's lots of things, but often, when we really want to perform well and stay motivated in the day-to-day, it boils down to knowing our 'why'. Simon Sinek wrote the book and did the TED Talk *Start with Why* a few years ago and he brought it back into mainstream thinking, but like many things, and with no disrespect to Simon, it was nothing new really. People have been talking about this for decades, and when I do a talk on motivation I have used the the 'Why', the 'How', and the 'Keeping On Going' for years now, long before his excellent book was popular. There are very few truly new ideas, mostly we do things that others have done or we make our own versions of it. George Lucas, I learned, even based Star Wars on a combination of westerns, mythical tales and a few very niche little movies that he loved. He just did his own version of those things and created something new. Anyway, I digress.

We were designed to work, but it helps if we know our 'why'. In fact, work is good for us. Have you ever been off work ill for few days? The first day is a novelty but then, after three days, you start to realise that daytime TV and not being able to go out of the house is not all it is cracked up to be. Work helps us to get out of the house and it pushes us into new experiences, both good and not so good. We all need to do things to pass time, earn money and keep us occupied.

Baseball

I love this story of a group of prisoners who found their 'why' very quickly…

In Wyoming State Prison in 1911 they formed a baseball team. Nothing remarkable about that; prisoners need occasional exercise. Except that this team was made up of men who were on death row.

In 1911 if you were sentenced to death, it would happen within a few months, nothing like the 10 or 20-year wait prisoners have today. So the new warden Felix Alston, who was a baseball obsessive, decided to set up the Wyoming State Prison All Star team. And this was the deal: if the team won, they were promised a stay of execution and if they lost, their execution date was to go ahead as normal! Chris Enss in her book, Playing for Time, tells the story of this bizarre set of games in the American West between 1911 and 1912.

Oh yes, that team was very motivated and they had found their 'why'. In fact, they won 39 games and only lost six. They were almost invincible over that 15 months. Not surprising really – they were playing for their lives, literally.

First aid

Ex-army Major, Jonathan Cunningham MBE, volunteers as a first responder to help paramedics in his local area. As part of that role he goes into primary schools and does first aid training with kids. One day in school he trained a young lad called Lucas. He was seven, and he got wrapped up in bandages along with his classmates learning how to do basic first aid.

Just a few hours after he'd done the training, Lucas saved his little sister's life. She was choking in the bath. Lucas alerted his Mum and then managed to stop his sister from choking, remembering what Jonathan had taught him. The story got into the papers and on the news and Jonathan was invited back to award a special certificate to Lucas.

When Jonathan got a text and a video message from Lucas saying what had happened he was delighted, as you could imagine. I asked Jonathan a few questions:

How did you feel when you heard what had happened?

"I was quite emotional and humbled to think that my simple training delivered to children had actually saved a life."

How did you feel when you delivered the next first aid session after the incident?

"I was energised, elated, proud and fuelled to deliver this training to as many children I possibly could."

Did you start to share Lucas' story when you were teaching first aid?

"Yes, everyone got to know about Lucas and his fast reactions in the bath to save his sister."

Even when I spoke to him on the phone, a few years after the incident, he was still smiling – you can always tell when people are. He really found his 'why' for this role; the fact that he indirectly saved a life inspires him now and drives him to continue to do his role well.

Do you have you those little moments in your job or life? Why do you do…? What difference have you made? Look for, remember and record those moments.

When we really want to perform well and stay motivated in the day-to-day it boils down to knowing our 'why'.

So, stop and think:

WHY do I go to work?

WHY do I do what I do?

WHY do I work there and not somewhere else?

WHY am I pursuing this dream/goal/project?

Push deeper into the why. Spend time and reflect on it.

About hard work

In our world of instant coffee, pot noodles and TV on demand, we can sometimes forget that not everything happens instantly. Have you ever tasted a Pot Noodle? You'll soon be hungry again. Instant sometimes just doesn't cut it. There's nothing better than a great home-cooked meal, that's why students go home for the holidays, I know, I had two.

When I first started researching hard work, I came across this seemingly obvious advice and I sort of wish it wasn't on my list. I wish I could say, "You'll just make it one day, it will all happen to you, you don't have to work hard, just chill at home – everything will be fine". It would make this section go viral, but, sadly, it just isn't true.

Everyone needs a hobby

I have two main hobbies – one is going into pound shops and asking how much things cost. If you live in London it's probably a £3 shop now, but here in Yorkshire we still have pound shops, at least at time of writing. I can spend hours in there talking to the staff and asking how much things cost, as they roll their eyes and radio security to get me removed from the building. "It's that bloke again asking how much things cost. Doesn't he know this is a pound shop?"

My other hobby is going into post offices and talking to random Yorkshire people. It's always amusing; sometimes they grunt at you, but often people chat in the way that northern people do. I was in the post office a few years ago chatting away to this lady in front of me. She was proper Yorkshire. I said, "Nice weather today? "Ah not so bad love, fair to middling" she said. She had a flat cap and a whippet – she was the full Yorkshire package right there in front of me.

So we were just chitchatting away about nothing in particular. Then, when she got to the front of the queue, she said to the guy behind the counter, "Can I have thirty scratch cards please?" and the guy pulled thirty scratch cards off that little wheel thing and handed them over to her. She paid the money and then this lovely Yorkshire lady suddenly turned into

Gollum from Lord of the Rings. She got a 10p piece out of her pocket and said quietly under her breath, "Ooh my precious" as she ran into the corner of the post office scratching away at the cards, hoping that something would happen to change her life. Her eyes got small and beady and she looked kind of angry as she was scratching away on her cards.

Then I had the real privilege of being present when she won… £10. Now, I'm no maths expert, but even I know that she's down on that day and of course the sad thing is that she goes in every day and does it again – hoping, praying, and scratching that something will change her life more than the £10 did. The odds against her winning are astronomical. Some sources say that to win £1million you'd have to buy £16million worth of scratch cards. She is probably more likely to be struck several times by lightning in the same place than she is to win a decent amount of money. But this lady and so many others, often out of desperation, are relying on someone else to change their lives. She's relying on unpredictable outside forces to change her life when really, over time, the best person to change our life is, of course, ourselves.

And that's where hard work comes in.

Working hard gets us from where we are now to where we want to be. It moves us forward, it passes time, we earn money and develop skills - it does all sorts of different things but it's not very exciting and it's certainly not newsworthy and is rarely reported in the media. Social media loves 99% of the time to ignore it completely - settling instead for amazing people doing amazing things without seeing the years and years of struggle, sweat, practice and hard work that went into them doing what they do best.

Batman and Robin

Now, it has to be said I don't look like a natural long distance runner, but one of my ambitions was to take part in the Great North Run in Newcastle. So one year I signed up and went from zero to running 13 miles in just a few months.

Let's be frank, running is for small and thin people, I was feeling a bit nervous, stood there all Vaselined up. When I got to the start line, there in front of me were Batman and Robin, both dressed up and dead keen, chatting away. They were local lads, and to be honest they looked like they'd had a skinful the night before, and they looked like they'd had a full English fried breakfast too. When the gun went off and we started to move, they ran off, at speed, and I thought this is not going to end well. A mile and a half down the road, as I was plodding along the tarmac I saw Batman and Robin at the side of the road huffing and puffing, looking like they were going to puke.

They weren't going to make it. But miraculously I did. Most of the training was boring, repetitive and sometimes even miserable but when, on the big day, I was struggling at 11 miles into the run as the big hill really kicked in, I was so glad I had done all that training. The slog, night after night running around Leeds in the rain, meant that when it came to the crunch I could finish the race. Working hard paid off when I needed it most. It is the same for my speaking too. As a speaker you can't replace working hard and simply getting on stage for, as the Americans call 'stage time' (imagine jazz hands at this point).

It's really unfashionable to talk about working hard and when I speak about this when I'm on stage I often talk about it being the two swear words: 'work hard'. I wish as a motivational speaker I didn't have to mention these words. I wish I didn't have to talk about them, but I wouldn't be telling the truth if I didn't.

There are loads of tips and tricks in this book that I hope will help you, but honestly our relationship with working hard, working smart and being resilient in tough or boring times is what gets the job done.

I'm sure most people reading this book don't need to be told by me to work hard, but I think it's good to reflect on.

- When do you work hard?
- Why do you work hard?
- What was one of the times where you worked the hardest?
- Maybe you can remember a time when you put off working hard and you procrastinated instead?

You may have hoped for someone else to step in and change your life, instead of the realisation that you can change your life by getting the right people around you and doing the right amount of work, on the right subject, so that you are in your element.

Hard work is rarely wasted – it might be ignored by a bad boss, or you might feel under appreciated working in a kitchen all day, but you're still earning money. Hopefully you're still learning some things, even if it's not the job you want to have in the longer term.

In his popular book *The Happiness Myth*, Dr. Russ Harris talks about the four myths of happiness. One of these is the myth that we should always be happy. This is where working hard can be lost. If we believe that we should be always happy, we won't understand the place that hard work has in our life. Some people's planning for their future is to cross their body parts, close their eyes and simply hope.

They'll buy a lottery ticket[21], or hope someone famous will pick them out of a crowd.I see people act like this. Even when my friend John Archer made it to the semi-finals of the big TV show *Britain's Got Talent*, they hardly mentioned that he had worked on his comedy magic for over 20 years before he was seen on that show.

Larry Page (one of the founders of Google) said: "You can't just have inspiration. It's maybe 10% inspiration and 90% perspiration". He was quoting the inventor Thomas Edison from 1903.

Some of the best people I know are the hardest working. Whether working in the public sector, a corporate, a local charity or in our own business - it's great to stop reflect and understand the impact of the work that we've done. Glance in the rear view mirror occasionally, celebrate what you have done. I will certainly be celebrating when this book is done. Celebrate the small, 'I have worked hard' victories before moving on.

I think about the thousands of hours of preparation I've done for talks, the thousands of hours delivering those talks and the thousands of people I

21 Weirdly, many big lottery winners have been called "Lottery Losers" because they wish they hadn't won the money after a while as it makes them very unhappy. Sad but true.

have met – none of that is wasted. Some of it was a bit boring, some was amazing, some was so-so. That's life, but I'm still gonna put the work in. I'm glad I put the work in; I'm glad I've worked hard between my periods of not working quite so hard.

I still remember the first real part-time job that I had, working in a fruit and veg shop. My teenage body was shocked at how early I had to be there, how cold it was in the winter and I wasn't particularly happy about being locked in the big fridge a few times by my so-called work friends either. But I was glad to learn something about retail, I'm glad I lifted the bags of potatoes and carrots and I met some fun people along the way. I knew that wasn't for me; I knew that shop wasn't going to be long-term for me, but I enjoyed it for a while and look back at it fondly now, realising that was the first time I really had to work hard.

I remember coming home from the first day and collapsing on the sofa, my Mam and Dad smiling at me, realising that I'd put in my first real work shift. If I remember rightly, they brought me soup for my tea on a tray in the living room. Pretty cute to be honest.

If any motivational speaker tells you that you don't have to work hard, run away.

Nothing you want to achieve in your life is going to happen without hard work. Work hard, but even better, work smart. Take breaks, have a day off, but earn it by having five or six days on. Work hard then reward yourself. As we say up north…"crack on", then have a cup of tea!

My sister once got told off by the boss of the building company who was renovating her house, because she kept giving the team bacon sandwiches first thing in the morning. "Stop giving them bacon," the boss said, "They don't get anything done otherwise." Work then reward worked better.

There are no short cuts to being successful at life and work. A lot of it is just working as hard and as smartly as we can, taking good advice along the way.

Work to your best ability – only you know deep down what that is for you.

Making dreams a reality

or why "follow your dreams" might just be the worst advice ever

As you may know by now, I have – over the years – played quite a bit of basketball; two or three times a week is pretty normal during the season. The stark reality is that when I play I'm often the oldest and the smallest guy playing – in fact sometimes I feel like I might be the smallest and oldest player in the UK. Until I started playing in the GB Masters veterans' tournament, then I felt positively sprightly as I played against guys in their 50s. I felt fast – well, for one weekend.

So why do I still play, especially when I come back with bumps, bruises, and aching limbs? Why do I keep turning up? Surely its time to hang up my Adidas boots and enrol to play carpet bowls? I am now, too, in my 50s after all. Well, maybe I'm too old to play now; some might say I just need to grow up, but the honest answer is that I love to play, I love scoring against the odds, and weirdly I love fighting for rebounds off guys way taller than me. And of course I like being part of a team, I like the banter. Also, chasing a bag of wind covered in leather around a court for 90 minutes makes me exercise way harder than in the often odd world of stark gyms with oiled men checking their biceps in the mirror and taking selfies after every set of chest presses. Gyms are too solitary for me.

I've been playing basketball since school and I love it, and being a big old school hip hop fan it's been part of my growing up. But here's the thing: it's a hobby. It's a pastime. It's my way of exercising, it helps me de-stress after a day of speaking or writing. It gets my brain out of my work, it keeps me fresh, it is a part of my life.

But here's the distinctive – I know I'm not particularly good, and I don't have any inclination to take it any further, apart from another occasional veterans' event. And I certainly don't think I could have ever been a pro like many players still believe deep down. I know my limitations in this area, and being 5'9" and chubby is definitely one of them.

Realising our potential, but also accepting limitations.

Don't get me wrong when I say this, I'm not being negative, but I think people still dream a lot about things that will never become a reality.

Maybe 'Follow your dreams', that now famous kitchen plaque, is just plain bad advice. Maybe it's even some of the worst advice we can get?

Let me try to make sense of it... If I dreamed of being an NBA basketball player – no matter how hard I worked, it just wouldn't happen. I'm too old, too short and too slow. That's a fact. Also it's true that only 25 players ever in the history of the NBA have been 5'9" or under!

But before you think I've turned into a grump, I haven't. I deal in, and speak about, reality and hope, not fairy tales and pipe dreams. To some people following a dream is just that – a daydream, no more, no less. As vital as dreams are for our brains and our creativity, we must learn to distinguish the difference between a pipe dream and a realistic aspiration.

I will always encourage someone to reach their potential, have a big aspiration or a stretch goal, whatever you want to call it. Why should we have small lives and tiny dreams?

But here's the thing – if we have a massive dream to see something happen in our lives, our work, or our communities, then we have to do certain things to make it happen, otherwise it is just a narcissistic pipe dream that can distract us and delay us from our real purpose in life.

There is nothing sadder than a person who keeps saying, "I could have been a contender, I could've been somebody", like Marlon Brando's character in *On The Waterfront* or Uncle Rico from the brilliant *Napoleon Dynamite*.

I meet people who talk about their past as if it will continue to shape or stop them forever. They also see no hope for the future. There is always hope, there is always a way to enjoy the journey of trying to turn a big dream into a reality. If we follow the right steps I've mentioned and not just dream, things can change for us.

So, let's make a real plan, don't just dream a pipe dream. We can really change the world, not just dream about it.

Here's my 'make a big dream a reality' checklist:

Firstly, write down your big dream...

In full bright high definition colour, sights, smells, feelings, everything – write it down and just think about it for a few days. Add to it, fill it out, let it 'marinate' in your head. After a few days, think – is this just a pipe dream or can it become a reality if I work at it?

Ask, can I physically do this thing?

If you are small and old like me becoming an NBA player isn't realistic. This doesn't mean that you can't do really 'big stuff', but sometimes there are real-life limitations, no matter what a well-meaning friend might tell you.

Have people validated you in this skill or job?

From the first public talk I ever gave, people said to me (and to my surprise), "You're pretty good at that, Lee". I still remember those words decades later, and that is one reason I now do what I do.

How do you feel when you think about this big dream?

Are you overwhelmed, nervous, or energised and excited at times? Passion for it is key, not essential, but very helpful, although don't get bound up waiting to 'feel like doing it', as often work is just that – work.

Share it with one or two very carefully selected friends...

...not any random family member and certainly not just negative people. Share it very carefully and wisely and get people's honest reactions. I do this. We should always filter feedback though – we don't have to accept it, but we should still listen to it.

Who does something similar?

Find out who and get to meet them, phone them or email them. My friend and researcher David Hyner knows of a UK school student who got through to speak to Barack Obama about a career in politics! People who have done something similar can save you months of hard work by helping you avoid expensive and time-wasting dead-end streets and dark alleys.

Hobby?

This sounds simple, but honestly I meet people who have lots of ideas for charities or business but the product or service just isn't sellable and so, sorry, it's a hobby not a business. Many businesses fail because they are in fact niche hobbies or passions. Some people love sticking seashells onto match boxes and selling them at craft fairs but no-one wants to buy them – that's a hobby.

If you feel that you want to go further – then start to chop up the big dream into tasks and goals and then put time aside in your diary to work on it. Even if you have a full time job – if this is something that you really want to do then you'll find time. I have never been a full-time author. If you love it or want it, you'll do it. I wrote four books while I had a full-time job and toddlers. We can make time for stuff.

Put in your diary to review this in 1, 3 and 6 months time. If you've made no progress, then you may need help, you need to make more time or, to be really honest, it's probably just a nice dream that may never see the light of day. That is OK by the way, we all have those, but it's the ones that we really work on that will see the light of day and change us or the world around us.

Make a realistic plan, don't just dream a dream and you can really change your life and the world, not just think about it.

The upside and downside of goal setting ... and getting stuff done

The veteran TV actor and star of *Doc Martin*, Martin Clunes was being interviewed on the BBC and was asked, "How did you get this new sitcom?" hinting at a decades-old mapped-out life plan and a visualised set goal that he had. He answered immediately, laughing and slightly bemused: "Oh, there's no master plan..."

He hadn't planned for this to happen and after a lifetime of TV acting roles he still doesn't really know how he gets the work he gets. His plan is that he's in the game, he's good at his job and available for work.

So it got me thinking about one of the most talked about things in the training world: goal setting.

For many decades now, the personal development industry has been based a lot around goal setting. I when I first got into this industry full-time (at time of writing, 15 years ago), I really tried hard to learn and get into prescriptive goal setting myself. I tried some goal setting programmes, and I just couldn't get on with them.

It was weird. I felt disconnected from goal setting.

I felt like it just didn't work for me and even after I'd paid for some goal setting books and programmes. I paid real money to try to make it work too. This often helps, as free stuff holds little value. But honestly, goal setting has never, in its traditional sense, ever sat right with me. And over the years I've come to understand that these programmes just don't mirror my values and maybe, my personality type. At the risk of offending my friends and colleagues in the industry, they are, in my opinion - not for everyone. Yes, you will hear me or have heard me talking about goals in this book on occasion. But when I talk about goals, I'm not talking about the traditional restrictive idea of goal setting that is often written about and repeated. Goals 'research' that is often quoted, but not actually true.

For instance, there is a mythical Harvard/Yale study on goal setting, it was one of the things that I heard about a lot initially, and still continue to hear today. The problem is, that that piece of research doesn't exist. Either in 1953 (Harvard), or 1979 (Yale). They didn't happen.

Many people have looked into this, they do not exist.

Now Harvard does, ironically, do research on goal setting. There's an excellent study called 'Goals Gone Wild' by a Professor of Business Administration at Harvard Business School. But there isn't the famous study where it says that the 3% of Harvard/Yale MBAs who wrote down their goals have made 10 times as much money as the other 97% combined. I've heard these percentages bandied around saying they are from the 50s, 60s or 70s, like they are facts that have been established many decades before.

This is proper fake news. It just is not true. Those figures and those studies simply do not exist. But they have been quoted in many books from leading people in the self-help and management consultancy industry.

When rumours like those happen, when fake news like that spreads, it can last for decades. You'll find thousands of references for these studies online. The Harvard and Yale study does not exist. Some goal setting studies do, of course, exist, but they're a little less convincing and, sadly for us all, a bit more complicated to communicate.

Even the often taught S.M.A.R.T. goal system made famous and attributed to massively influential business writer Peter Drucker, is actually research from George T Dorin from 1981. Dorin's original but concise article makes interesting reading[22], even warning of overthinking, over-measuring and quantifying.

In the 'Goals Gone Wild' study[23], they encourage us to think differently. The goal setting techniques often replicated and very influential in hundreds of books, are very black and white, highly measured and outcome-focused, often money-driven and external or extrinsic in nature. Nobody really looks at the downside of goal setting.

The study says that prescriptive goal setting gives us a very narrow focus, so we can miss the bigger picture. For example, in the Covid pandemic, if as a speaker my main goal was to speak to a big crowd or audience in, say, the Royal Albert Hall, that just could not happen, it was shut – so it would make me feel like a failure.

Goals can neglect non-goal areas like relationships, so we can be very focused on, say, a financial goal, but ruin our families and friendships in the process.

Goals can see a rise in unethical behaviour. People can start to cheat to achieve goals, steal sales from colleagues or cheat the system[24] and it can

22 Original article is here:
https://community.mis.temple.edu/mis0855002fall2015/files/2015/10/S.M.A.R.T-Way-Management-Review.pdf

23 Goals Gone Wild: The Systematic Side Effects of Over-Prescribing Goal Setting by Lisa D. Ordóñez, Maurice E. Schweitzer, Adam D. Galinsky and Max H. Bazerman

24 https://www.psu.edu/news/research/story/middle-managers-may-turn-unethical-behavior-face-unrealistic-expectations/ Poortvliet, Marijn & Darnon, Céline. (2010). Toward a More Social Understanding of Achievement Goals. Current Directions in Psychological

even "start the corrosion of organisational culture" – pretty serious stuff, often in the news.

The studies also noted the reduced value of intrinsic (internal) motivation – motivators that more of us have, like wanting to achieve well, have job satisfaction and feel like we are making a difference for our clients, customers or connections.

"On the basis of investigations in various sub-disciplines of psychology, we conclude that mastery goals – striving to improve one's own performance – lead to investments in exchange relationships, endorsement of reciprocity norms, and active efforts to integrate different opinions. In contrast, performance goals – striving to outperform others – may result in rather maladaptive social behaviors."[25]

If we only rely on external validation (in this case external prescriptive goals) for our work, dreams etc, it can be demotivating. Most people do not respond well to a big old fashioned dry-wipe sales board.

We do have to measure things, that is business and it makes sense, but that is very different from personal or work-based one-way prescriptive goals at the expense of everything else.

So why are prescriptive goals taught so much?

I think some management teams like the idea of these simple goals strategies. They pay for the training on them because they are easy to understand, it gives them more perceived daily 'control'. They are fooled by the false research that they love, or that they think that people are all motivated in the same way. A big mistake to make as a leader or a manager.

So with all this in mind, how should we approach goals, and what do I mean by goals?

Science - CURR DIRECTIONS PSYCHOL SCI. 19. 324-328. 10.1177/0963721410383246.
25 Poortvliet, Marijn & Darnon, Céline. (2010). Toward a More Social Understanding of Achievement Goals. Current Directions in Psychological Science - CURR DIRECTIONS PSYCHOL SCI. 19. 324-328. 10.1177/0963721410383246.

1. **Not everything needs a goal**

   "You have to be very careful when you apply goals" is great advice.

2. **Think compass, not GPS**

   As many writers[26] say, think of a goal as a compass giving you a direction, rather than a specific destination or path with a GPS end to it. That is much more helpful. If we have a compass we can go in the direction that we need to go and enjoy the journey along the way, without that restrictive, pinpoint location that some people feel they need to map out every day, week, month, and year. This can easily be demotivating because, if we miss one of those markers, we can feel like we've lost it all. This is easily seen if people are trying to lose weight. They miss one day and can then lose the plot, eat a massive tub of Ben and Jerry's and stop eating well. Whereas if we have a direction of travel and are going in the right direction, that really helps.

3. **Discipline is key, not just goals**

   I also like the idea that we can always overestimate what we can do in a year, but underestimate what we can do in five years. My work certainly is a testimony to that. I thought things would happen much quicker than they actually did. But when I look back over the last few years I can see how things have developed at the right time and in the right direction for me. But they've developed in a good direction, and not to a specific GPS goal.

   In a BBC article[27] about goals they quote a great example of how this can be used wrongly. One company set a goal for its call centre employees to keep their call times under two minutes in order to get more calls done. That was translated into workers picking up the phone, dialling somebody and then putting the phone down within two seconds. So on the whiteboard, they'd rung more people, but of course they hadn't achieved the real goal, which was to talk with

26 https://www.fastcompany.com/3029765/how-to-set-goals-for-the-life-you-actually-want

27 https://www.bbc.com/worklife/article/20171117-why-we-should-all-give-up-on-goals-already

more customers and to make more sales.

Traditional goals can be misunderstood. They can even be demotivating. They can feel restrictive and people can feel like they're on a never-ending treadmill.

So when we talk about goals, think more about the direction of travel. Also, where does your, or your organisation's, purpose fit too? "We're going here at the moment", "We're going in that direction" – this will reduce the feeling of failure.

4. **You're probably not a teenager anymore**

Don't wish for something now that you only wanted back then. We are complex human beings. We can't write out a timed plan for our life. Imagine if you've written a goal down aged 18 and now you're 55. Did you want your whole life to be run like you thought it should be run when you were 18? I certainly don't. I was all about hip-hop DJ-ing in those days and, even though I had fun, I'd hate being that person now.

There's probably nothing sadder than a guy in his 50s shouting, "Jump up, jump up – put your hands in the air" to a crowd of clubbers. A lot has happened since then. While it's fantastic to hear of people like Nicola Adams saying that she wanted to be a Olympic champion, she said that at age 13. She set a great direction of travel, but did she have a mapped-out set of smart interim goals that you could tick off on a sheet? I don't know, but we do achieve by keeping the direction. Sometimes we can turn something that should be fun into drudgery through rigid and specific timed goals.

There is some evidence that written goals can increase performance and can motivate people, and we can see that in the famous Locke study[28] in the 60s, although I'm still not convinced that's for everyone and the fact that 95% of organisations use them without asking, "Do they work?" is a concern.

1968 was a long time ago – neuroscience, personality profiling and psychology has moved on in leaps and bounds since then. I'm

28 Edwin A. Locke, Toward a theory of task motivation and incentives, *Organizational Behavior and Human Performance*, Volume 3, Issue 2, 1968

concerned that a rigid set goal makes itself a selfish god. Everyone runs around after it and, by hook or by crook and sometimes with unethical behaviour, people try to please their written-down god goal.[29]

Whereas with the compass philosophy – set your compass, go in the right direction, lay down some markers, and if things change along the way – it's not the end of the world. Keep an eye on your compass and keep going in that direction. That can make a big difference to our personal motivation levels without the constant failure built into traditionally measured goal setting programmes.

5. **Goals also can be cute and easy to manage, but are they realistic?**

   They're handy for managers to see on their spreadsheet or whiteboard, they can make a cute tin plaque to put on our kitchen walls, but really – is that what life and work is like, being that inflexible? I think life is partly learning from the cul-de-sacs, but also enjoying the occasional side roads and the people you meet along the way. It's not just a single pinpoint GPS destination. I mean, life literally is to enjoy the journey.

So remember:

- Use goals to suit your personality
- Think about goals creatively
- Think about them in a way that inspires you, rather than making you feel like a prisoner
- Be truly accountable
- Enjoy the direction of travel on the way to whatever your future may look like

29 Mike Morrison from RapidBI (who's looked extensively into the myth of the "they wrote them down" Harvard/Yale studies at length) points towards a small study from the Dominican University of California in 2007, which looks at the effectiveness of accountability, commitment and writing down goals. Their findings are only a small group though, and only over four weeks, but this just isn't the big long study that we need. https://web.archive.org/web/20100527213612/http://www.dominican.edu/academics/ahss/psych/faculty/fulltime/gailmatthews/researchsummary2.pdf

QUICK WINS

Are you an innie or an outie?

Human motivation is very complex, but it comes from two basic places. Where do you get your motivation from?

Intrinsic motivation

...is personal and internal. It's rewarding to you personally.

For example:

"I play football, because I love it."

"I'm reading this book because I like this author."

"I tidy my office to make me feel organised and clean."

"I enjoy studying."

Extrinsic motivation

...is a push, a pull, or is reward-based, or it is simply avoiding failure.

For example:

"I play football to lose weight."

"I am reading this for a presentation that I've got coming up."

"I tidy my office, because there's a visitor coming round."

"I am revising for an exam."

Neither is right or wrong. They're just different.

Find out the way that you're motivated most – try and work out how you tick. It helps you understand others more too. Are you more intrinsic or extrinsically motivated – at work? At home?

Put another way - are you an 'innie' or an 'outie'?

Are you mainly internally motivated or externally motivated? Nothing to do with your belly button, but to do with your character and personalty.

Have a think, stop and reflect: where do I get my motivation from, and how can that help me?

Be present

Don't spend your time at work thinking about your holidays and then your time on holiday thinking about work. Find a way to be present in both of those places.

Sometimes we get it mixed up. Actually, when we're at work we need to be thinking about work, and when we're on our holiday, we need to be enjoying that holiday. The grass is not greener in other places; sometimes we just have to be where we are.

As leadership and communications speaker Nigel Risner says "If you're in the room - be in the room". Yup, if you're in the office be in the office, if you're on holiday, be on holiday.

Easy to say, harder to maintain, but helpful to us in the long term.

Get the full picture

While writing this book I've been gathering together some old videos and audio tapes ready to get them transferred into digital files before they disintegrate. Yes, I am that old. I'm glad I did too, as our wedding video has already started to look a bit wobbly! (Ask an old person about VHS tracking at this point if you're under the age of 30.)

The other thing I noted is that some of the tapes we have are obviously copies of copies. A copy of an analogue video or audio tape is always slightly worse quality, and then when that is copied and copied it gets to the point where it sounds and looks terrible.

All copies get worse over time.

I'm a big believer in learning from others. Looking up to people or, as they say, looking 'into' people[30], can be a great way of learning skills and building expertise.

When I first started as a speaker, I spent the first few months buying coffee for as many speakers as I could get in touch with. Some of those kind people are still friends today many years later. But, and there's a big but – we should never copy others. Learn from them. But don't copy them. Especially if you are viewing them from afar or via social media.

One of the reasons we shouldn't copy 'successful' people is because we really don't know what it cost them to get what they got. We always see a heavily edited version.

30 A phrase made famous by athlete and speaker Kriss Akabusi

They are almost certainly cropping out some stuff – the 'influencer' using pills to keep them going, a leader who is an angry bag of nerves before a talk, the comedian who slept in their car for weeks, just to get an open spot gig to start their career.

TV and films don't help – they show life with all the boring bits taken out! It's very rare to see someone do their tax return in a film or see an actor running to the loo five times just before their play starts. Copying others through the lens of distance never gives the full picture.

A friend of mine was fascinated by a visiting foreign speaker and went to see them quite a few times when they were in his area, but after a while he realised that they only had two or three stories that got repeated wherever they went. The picture of their life they painted in their talks was true, but it was highly edited.

Don't be tempted to copy others, look at them, learn from them but find your own voice, style and values.

There's no one else like you, and that's kind of the point.

On purpose

Maybe the most famous book on attitude and purpose is *Man's Search For Meaning: The classic tribute to hope from the Holocaust* by Viktor E Frankl.

Frankl, an eminent psychiatrist by profession, spent time in Auschwitz, the Nazi concentration camp, during World War Two. The book tells about his time in the camp, and how he saw hope and purpose emerge in the most horrendous situation imaginable. Certainly worth a read or a listen.

Self-belief

Right in the middle of the Harry Potter film The Order of the Phoenix, Harry says "Working hard is important, but there's something that matters even more, and it's believing in yourself."

- Do you really believe in your abilities or attitude?
- Do you believe that you can and do make a difference?
- Do you believe that you can make a workplace or community better?
- Who else believes in you?

Even if you can't believe in yourself, find someone else that can help and will believe in you – or learn and find ways to believe in yourself. One of the reasons I find that people don't reach for big dreams and sometimes don't work really hard, is because they simply don't believe in themselves.

We all need an element of belief in ourselves, with regular reminders from our inner self, a notebook or other people.

Belief in yourself is important, but with our history, hurt and often feelings of being an imposter it is, for some, not easy at all.

Here are a few ways to help build your self-belief:

- Decide what you know you are good at. No matter how small
- Think about the good relationships that you have
- Develop a good positive habit, like a gratitude list, daily
- Become deliberately less critical of yourself, ie look for the good in the day you've just had, not only the bits that went wrong
- Get the help you need, whether it is coffee with a good friend who can listen to you or professional talking therapies such as Cognitive Behavioural Therapy (CBT)
- Learn more about boundaries and start saying no more often to create time for yourself
- Also, look at your diary and put in some fun stuff EVERY week - before the boring things

Ikigai

The concise (and useful) Japanese Ikigai[31] diagram that did the rounds online a few years ago, it turns out, was actually devised in Guernsey by a coach called Marc Winn. Winn blogged about it, it went viral and then was featured in a best-selling book by two other authors. Ikigai (roughly meaning 'a reason for being' amongst other translations) in Japan is a whole lifestyle and deeper philosophy on happiness and purpose.

Even with its origins not wholly being what we may have thought, it is actually a very useful tool when thinking about purpose and careers. Not always doable of course – but a nice guide as we think and reflect on our work over time. Where are you at the moment?

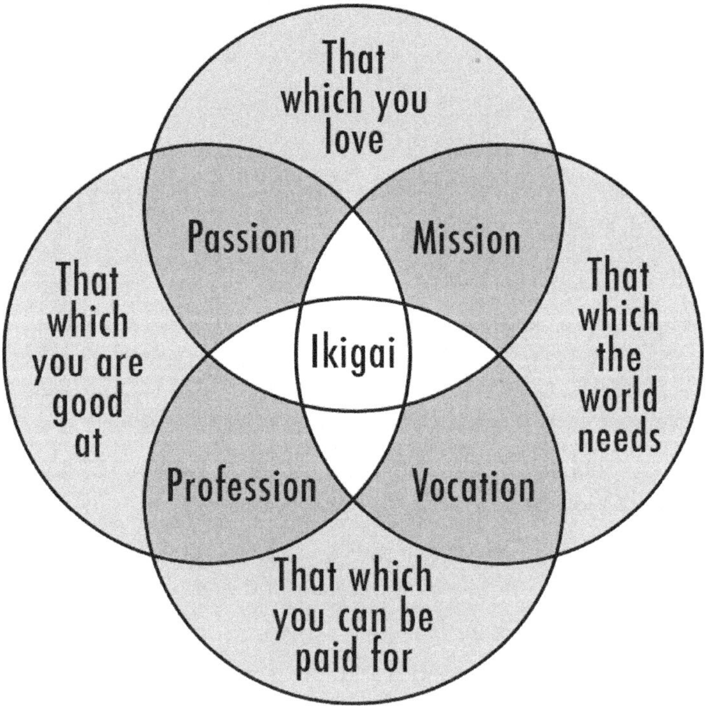

31 Pronounced ik-e-guy. Source: https://theviewinside.wpengine.com/what-is-your-ikigai - also see 02:50 on this video too: https://www.youtube.com/watch?v=a_2Rlydy_NQ

A quick word about faith and belief

Sometimes we can clearly see people's belief systems by what they wear, what they say, or what they do - but sometimes they can be hidden. However they may or may not manifest, it's important for us to understand faith, belief systems and philosophies a little bit and not think they are irrelevant to motivation.

A good leader who has a faith or religion needs to understand other people's world views, and a good leader who would say they have no beliefs also needs to understand other peoples world views too.

Some people's faith and belief systems are very deep personal motivators. It is important to recognise and understand that, no matter what our beliefs may be.

Having a bad day?

It usually isn't. Challenging – but true.

We all have bad stuff happen to us. Sometimes more than one bad thing in a day too, and yes, that wears us down. I have had those kind of days. I am not denying the reality of life.

What I've realised is, what makes a bad day is usually me. My attitude, my ruminating on it, repeating it to everyone I see. But also in not taking responsibility for my attitude.

A bad day could change into a good day very easily.

- Someone might give you a wedge of money. That might help.
- Your best friend could call you with good news. That would be nice.
- You see a really funny video on social media and makes you laugh out loud.

We shouldn't always have our mood or happiness directly attached with string to good or bad external things. That creates an exhausting life.

Anyway, string is hard to hold for long periods of time, it burns our fingers.

Attitude is the ultimate in free will, it is a choice we make: a minute-by-minute choice on a bad day.

Have a short moan, have a good shrug, blow out you cheeks and then choose your attitude for the rest of the day – occasionally through gritted teeth.

Motivation to exercise

"I can never get myself out for a run – I am so de-motivated."

There are no 100% certain solutions to motivation in situations like this, as everyone is different. But, as we mention elsewhere – habits are good. When I used to run I put my runs in my diary like they were work appointments, that really helped me. I trained for, and ran two half marathons that way, and trust me – I am not a natural long distance runner. Now my basketball sessions are diary appointments too.

If you wait for motivation it never arrives. In all honesty, get dressed, get your music on and kick yourself out of the door. Or get someone else to kick you out of the door!

But then, more importantly, remember after you have run, that you have done it. Maybe even write yourself a note or record a video after the run telling yourself: "we did it" – "I feel good"– "it is good for you" etc.

Talk to yourself more and give yourself an occasional kick: it works for me and is pretty solid with the research I've done.

No room for guilt in life. Find what works for you. Get out there.

The Coach

Coach John Wooden was one of the first true leadership experts in my opinion. He was a great coach and leader.

My paraphrase of his main message is this:

'Success is peace of mind in knowing that you did your best to become the best that you are capable of becoming'.

Reminder 4387 to never compare yourself to other people – they're different, they're made differently, their insides are different, their brain is wired differently. But the real reason to never compare yourself to anyone else, is so that you can be the best that you can be.

There's only one Lee Jackson in the world with my DNA, thankfully. I'm the only one, and I'm going to try to be the best Lee Jackson that I can be.

Someone might even have the same name as me, but they aren't me, so only I can be the best that I can be. I will stumble and I will fail, but I will still give it a good go.

The positive and negatives of gaming

I was working with a website development company recently, and one manager was asking me for some advice about a member of his team who was particularly unmotivated and seemed to be always distracted, constantly checking his phone.

I don't have much time for video games these days, but when I was a teenager I played loads on my little computer. I used to love it. It got me thinking of modern device gaming, as this manager was struggling to comprehend the performance of his team member. Amongst the generation entering the workplace now some are full-on, lifelong gamers. The global average now for a binge gaming session duration is 5.1 hours.[32] Many play for longer and often well into the night, becoming almost nocturnal, but still have to get up for work, school or college. Gaming can teach us many things including persistence, but there is downside to it from a motivational angle.

Here's what I think is the problem: we get rewarded in a video game, usually quite often. Whenever we finish a level, kill an enemy, win a race or even come third, we win a cup or we get some stars or gems. Then there's a power-up of some sort; we become stronger or get better weapons, and there is a satisfying high-pitched 'bing' noise or a cash register or ammo 'ker-ching'.

Obviously life isn't really like that.

So, my concern is that people can get addicted to that constant dopamine rush of gaming and so can unwittingly transfer that experience and think that they should be rewarded all the time at work and in life.

Sometimes we just have to get your head down and get our job done, it is good to get verbal encouragement from others – it is good to be built up – but sometimes that doesn't come, and we all need to learn to find ways to be productive and resilient, without the need to be rewarded or encouraged externally every few minutes with content, messages, or likes.

32 https://www.statista.com/statistics/936732/consecutive-time-spent-playing-video-games-worldwide/

Values

Rather than waiting to feel motivated (which rarely happens), more and more psychologists are encouraging us to let our values lead, not your feelings.

We hardly ever feel like doing stuff, but our values can become the driver, if we let them. Some say that a lot of stress is also caused by acting outside of our values.

Doing what is important to us in our heart will help us to get, or stay, more motivated. I just spoke to a dog breeder about a dog we were thinking about. She was so passionate about her dogs and the 5-star breeder rating she has, she apologised to me for not replying to my email sooner. I told her that I didn't want her to respond to my email sooner. I want her looking after her dogs – that is why she was recommended.

She said she is never motivated to do admin. I know the feeling, but I'd rather she was a day late replying to emails than neglecting the dogs in her care.

Meg Selig in a blog[33] on the *Psychology Today* website says:

"Knowing your values can guide your actions and give you inner peace."

She goes on to say: "...If you are not sure about your own core values, or if you would like to clarify which of your values are top priority now, choose your top six to eight values from a wide-ranging list. To do this, you need a good list – there are many out there but just use the mini-list that follows if you like, making good use of the 'other' options at the end of the list... It's natural to modify some of the values on this list as you face new and challenging situations. However, other values represent enduring ideals that you would only change under duress."

33 Meg Selig (http://megselig.com) used with kind permission: https://www.psychologytoday.com/us/blog/changepower/201811/6-ways-discover-and-choose-your-core-values

Financial Security	*Learning*
Compassion	*Leadership*
Health/Fitness	*Survival*
Nature	*Self-Preservation*
Accomplishment	*Security*
Creativity	*Adventure*
Dependability	*Family*
Loyalty	*Work*
Beauty	*Success*
Bravery	*Calm*
Gratitude	*Freedom*
Love	*Other*___
Connection/Relationships	*Other*___

Become values-led and enjoy becoming the sort of person you want to be.

Let your values motivate you, so if you feel tired, stressed or miserable, you can still do what matters. You can still get stuff done. It is a great long-term goal to switch from being feelings-led to being values-led.

There are many values inventories online and in books. It would definitely be worth your time if you have never done one.

> The nature of life is not permanence, but flux.
>
> ***Carson, Downton Abbey***

4

How to keep on going

Resilience:

'The capacity to recover quickly from difficulties; toughness'.

Persistence:

'...continuing in an opinion or course of action in spite of difficulty or opposition'.

The problem with writing about resilience is that it is so easy to misunderstand it or make it all about being permanently '100% motivated', 'feeling amazing' and easily 'pushing through' every obstacle we face.

It's not that.

While thinking a lot about this subject that I love, and looking at the research I've gathered and written down over the years - I am now fully convinced that we can't talk about resilience or persistence without talking about wellbeing at the same time.

Resilience and wellbeing should go hand in hand and they should be taught hand in hand too.[34]

In this section I'll give you some quick wins and deeper dives on the whole subject of resilience, persistence, or as I call it: 'keeping on going'...

---

34 There is a third thing here: there should be some responsibility from an employer around resilience too. We cannot expect individuals to be ever-increasingly resilient, we do have to make a job manageable in the long term, particularly as people all have different levels of resilience and capacity.

Misdirection and myths

Some people do annoyingly appear to be 'naturally resilient' and never seem to stop or suffer real setbacks. I'm sure there are a few of these people somewhere, but in the real world, 99.9% of the time I don't think that's true – it is just that we don't hear everyone's inner voices and inner workings. We don't have access to what is going on inside their heads.

This is a deep subject with many grey areas, and this is where I get concerned, as a speaker and researcher on the fashions, trends and sometimes myths surrounding personal and professional resilience.

For example - there is no doubt that our diet will make a difference to our wellbeing. That is undeniable. Ask anyone who has lived on pizza for a whole year.

Rubbish in, rubbish out.

But there is very little evidence to show that wacky, strict, and frankly, odd foods and diets will make us more resilient.[35] Nor will randomly jumping into an ice hole. I have nothing against jumping into ice holes – you feel free, I'll stay here in my centrally heated house – but, seriously - be careful, people can die doing that type of thing. Plus, we underestimate the support given to individuals undertaking these types of activities that we see on TV. The deep counselling or therapy that surrounds things like that is more important than the wacky diets or ice plunges. They won't do much alone, we'd just get cold, or hungry, and they can be dangerous. Sadly, I know of more than one person who has died because of their obsession with extreme diets and so-called 'detoxing'.[36]

There are no easy steps to relentless resilience. I wish there was. These big claims make great book, speech and YouTube titles, but they rarely are true. Or at least, they rarely are the full picture.

35 So many new foods on the market claim to boost our health in many ways: https://www.thegrocer.co.uk/trend-reports/from-soaring-sales-to-growing-cynicism-how-immune-supporting-claims-are-shaping-food-and-drink-npd/654622.article

36 Doctors say that detoxing the body is impossible, it just doesn't work: https://www.theguardian.com/lifeandstyle/2014/dec/05/detox-myth-health-diet-science-ignorance

Resilience, like many concepts in life, is beautifully complex and nuanced and there are lots of contrasting opinions out there.

Shouty

The other thing I see sometimes in the personal development resilience space is the hard-core shouty personalities, often ex-miltary guys in camo (and it's usually guys) who advocate pushing ourselves to our absolute limits and then beyond.

These people can go viral and write books that look exciting, but the reality can be very different. Some of the amazing people that I know who have served in the military and have lived this lifestyle in wartime eventually burned out, and some suffer from post-traumatic stress disorder. Their health and even their personalities can be affected by their wartime experiences, so we must be responsible in this area.

One of these guys, after many years, eventually admitted his serious struggles with his mental health. I don't want to mirror the habits and lifestyle of a shouty person advocating CEOs and managers to scream at employees and display other sociopathic behaviours. I am not wired that way, and it is not healthy for the learner or their team.

It's a delicate balance, and I'm sure I don't get it all right. I hope you know yourself what the balance between pushing hard and wellbeing needs to be for you.

So here are my tips, tricks and reflections on resilience - not in any strict reading order. Dip in, dip out. Eat the meat and spit out the bones. Stop, reflect, take notes and make this relevant for you and your stage of life right now.

Whether you are facing your first big challenge in a few weeks time, or leading a multi-million pound organisation every day, there is something here for you.

DEEP DIVE

The reality check

Life isn't all sweetie shops and candy canes.

Even writing this book, I realise that people love to romanticise writing It's not like the film *Love Actually*, where the character is writing a novel overlooking a private lake, tapping away on a cool-looking vintage typewriter and weighing down the perfectly formatted manuscript with a small polished rock to save it from the gentle breeze.

Sorry. This is my 13th book. Most days writing a book is a bit like walking into a dark cave with a bag full of ideas and a small torch - with enough battery for about 90 minutes of light a day.

And as much I love the outcome of a book and helping people - I rarely enjoy the process, and there is never a convenient time to write. I just have to find my way around my work, family and distractions - celebrating the little victories along the way and keep myself going until it is done.

When I started tackling resilience in my talks years ago I started collecting stories of people who had gone further, failed often and pushed harder than most.

It is a great reminder that most things are hard fought for.

Famously, Walt Disney had to go to 302 different banks before he could get a bank loan for Disneyland.[37] I went to the newer Disney World to a big conference, and it seemed like his company now owns half of Florida – it is enormous. But no one would give him a bank loan to start a theme park, probably because no one had ever done it before. So that meant that 301 times he got up, got dressed, went to a meeting and they said

37 Annoyingly this number cannot be fully sourced or proven. But given his long-term relationship with Bank of America who funded lots of his big films, it is highly likely that he searched for many years for money for Disneyland from banks and financiers, particularly after his breakdown. https://www.wdw-magazine.com/was-there-a-bank-inside-disney-land

, "No thanks". But eventually he did get the money, and the Disney empire started. What if he'd stopped at 299?

Do you have a KFC in your town or city? The co-founder, Colonel Harland Sanders, got in his car, penniless, aged 65 and went, as legend has it, to 1,009 different restaurants before someone would try out his secret recipe and pressure-cooked-style chicken we eat today. So,1,008 times, he got rejected. He learned the value of keeping on going.

Along with hundreds of musicians, authors, entrepreneurs and activists, Colonel Sanders learned that failures are all part and parcel of success. They are signposts along the road. U2 and Madonna were rejected rudely, two of the most influential bands/musicians in the world. Harry Potter author JK Rowling was rejected 12 times by major UK publishers; she even keeps one of those letters framed on her kitchen wall.

Just taking authors alone, some of the biggest authors and books in the world were rejected out of hand, including:

- Agatha Christie
- Jack Canfield & Mark Victor Hansen – *Chicken Soup for the Soul*
- J.D. Salinger - *The Catcher in the Rye*
- Dr Seuss
- L.M. Montgomery – *Anne of Green Gables*
- *The Tale of Peter Rabbit* by Beatrix Potter was turned away, so she self-published 250 copies. It has sold over 45 million,
- Margaret Mitchell's *Gone With The Wind* was rejected 38 times. It sold over 30 million.
- *Narnia* creator C.S. Lewis
- *The Diary of Anne Frank* was seen as "not remarkable" - it sold 25 million.
- "That will never sell" – *The Wind In The Willows* by Kenneth Grahame. It has sold 25 million.
- Wm Paul Young self-published his novel *The Shack* after 20 rejection letters. It became a big hit with over 15 million sold.
- Meg Cabot got rejected many times, but *The Princess Diaries* sold over 15 million copies.

- *The Lord Of The Flies*? Rejected.
- *The Color Purple*, rejected, sold 10 million and won the Pulitzer Prize.
- *The Time Traveler's Wife* by Audrey Niffenegger was rejected 25 times but sold seven million.
- "I received sixty rejections", Kathryn Stockett said of her worldwide hit *The Help*.
- Five publishers rejected *Life of Pi* by Yann Martel. It won The Booker Prize in 2002.
- *The War Of The Worlds* by H.G. Wells and *Moby Dick* by Herman Melville? Rejected.
- Louisa May Alcott refused to give up on her novel *Little Women*. It is still around 140 years later.
- *Catch-22* by Joseph Heller is an interesting one, it was rumoured he called it that because the 22nd publisher said yes to him. Now over 10 million sold.
- Even L Frank Baum's *The Wonderful Wizard Of Oz* was a reject!

I'll stop.[38] You get the gist.

The ultimate driving test

But even with these big impressive lists and many other rejection emails and letters posted online, my favourite story of rejection and persistence is still one I found in 2009 and was covered on many news websites.[39] It tells of a woman called Cha Sa-soon from near Seoul in South Korea. In 2009, she passed her written driving test.

Nothing spectacular about that. Except she had taken it 950 times.

---

38 Online there are pages and pages of these kind of lists. Here are two good sources: http://www.litrejections.com/best-sellers-initially-rejected/ - a great website encouraging writers to keep going! Also https://lithub.com/the-most-rejected-books-of-all-time/

39 https://www.reuters.com/article/idUKIndia-38133620090221
http://news.bbc.co.uk/1/hi/ 8347164.stm#:~:text=A%20South%20Korean%20woman%20is,needed%20to%20pass%20the%20test.
https://www.koreaherald.com/view.php?ud=20100809000511
https://www.nytimes.com/2010/09/04/world/asia/04driver.html

Unlike the Disney and KFC stories that are legend but unproven, this one is. Yep, it was reported and verified, she took it 950 times.

That means that she got up, took two buses, sat at the desk, got a pen out and took her written driving test 949 times and each time they said she had failed.

Not even, "You nearly passed", not a "Well done, you smasher!" It was a simple pass or fail and she failed – a lot.

949 times. Impressive.

Cha Sa-soon became a bit of a celebrity in South Korea and Hyundai put her in a car advert and gave her a free car for her resilience. Grandma Cha Sa-soon, as she became known, is quite rightly a legend. It was reported that there was a note on a wall in her house, next to the photo of her late husband, that simply said, "Don't give up". She certainly didn't.

I think in Southeast Asia they celebrate persistence and resilience maybe more than we do here in the UK. All countries' cultures have their strengths and weaknesses. No country is perfect, and I certainly saw that when we went to Japan. I did notice how hard people worked there. Kids were in school longer. People worked harder, they celebrated hard work – or you could say they celebrate overwork, but in this context I really think it is a deep cultural thing.

I sometimes think here in the UK that our prevailing culture, no matter our background is, "You've tried it once, leave it". "Don't try it again". "Don't embarrass yourself". That is certainly not what Cha Sa-soon did.

Once we see through the filters and sanitised view of success - achievement in the cold light of day is about failure. Whether we get up from it or whether we give up from it.

As mentioned in a New York Times article on this story, the Korean world champion boxer Hong-Su-hwan made popular the idea in 1977 of *saj eon ogi* – which means 'knocked down four times, rising up five'.

That is at the heart of resilience - not denying the knocks but encouraging, planning for, and working towards the getting up.

Ways to get back up again

Let's talk about our feelings.

I was listening to a comedian the other day and he really made me laugh when he said, "Have you ever had a really random thought that just comes out of nowhere?"

"I was driving down the M1 the other day," he said, "and suddenly I thought I wonder what would happen if I turned the wheel now and rammed into that central barrier?"

People in the audience laughed nervously, because we all have random thoughts from time to time, but thankfully most of the time we don't act on them. That is the most important bit, and proves that we are doing well, so psychologists say.

Phew.

A random thought or feelings is perfectly normal and thankfully they do not define us. Our thoughts and feelings are very important - they are part of what makes us who we are.

My daughters are officially 'identical' – so, as identical twins, surely they feel the same, right? Well, they look pretty similar and, with the exception of feeling hungry and occasionally filling their nappies at the same time when they were very little, their thoughts and feelings have always been different.

Even though they look similar, they're not the same, they are unique. They have similar, but ever-so-slightly different DNA. (Identical twins are thought to be born with identical DNA but it can change over time often as they grow.[40])

But here's the reality about our thoughts and feelings. We are not ruled by them, we shouldn't listen to ALL of them and here's the big thing: we can flip them and change them too.

When our favourite song comes on the radio, it can really change the way we feel. If we are in public we might tap our fingers or move our

40 https://www.pnas.org/doi/full/10.1073/pnas.0500398102

feet, we might even smile, but if we are at home in the kitchen we might even grab a spatula to sing out loud or do a little cheesy dance. I have. Come on admit it, you have too – especially if you thought no-one was watching. If we were controlled by our every thought and feeling, we'd do terrible things or maybe just not do anything at all.

- It's better to build our lives on facts not feelings.
- Facts are like standing on concrete.
- Feelings are like trying to stand on a cloud.

Take my area – public speaking – as an example. I once coached someone who could hardly stand up and even say their name in a group without going to pieces. They came on my speaking course and I was asked to help them with some extra sessions too. In those sessions, using speaking as the reason to be there, I basically helped them to control their negative thoughts and got them into a better thought routine. Once we had done that, everything started to change.

They changed their thought patterns and that in turn changed their feelings, and then of course it affected their actions for the better.

They went on to nail an important speech in front of an audience in the houses of parliament, something they thought just wasn't possible a few weeks beforehand.

Habits, routines and disciplines

We all have routines, even if we think we haven't. Some of our routines are good, but some are, for various reasons, faulty.

We clean our teeth on a morning without thinking about it. That's a routine.

We drive to work or back home without thinking about it sometimes and 'wake up' when we arrive. That's a routine too.

Be a little more aware of your thoughts and your feelings. They are important, but we aren't defined by them and we can make positive changes to the sometimes random and often negative thoughts that we have.

We aren't designed to live 'under our bad thoughts' inside of bad routines. We can live life more fully. Get some help, talk to others, learn to notice, grab, flip and replace those bad thoughts, then watch as your new routine gradually starts to make you feel more confident.

In fact I'll stick my neck out here and say that if we want to get good at anything, and want to keep on going more effectively, it always boils down to these three main things:

- **Habits**
- **Routines**
- **Disciplines**

Need to learn to swim? It'll require a new habit of taking lessons, a new weekly routine of going swimming and maybe some books to read, videos to watch and exercises to do. It'll be a new discipline, at least for a while.

Want to become more productive in your work day? It'll require some new habits, definitely a new routine to stay on task and indeed, more discipline or disciplines.

The problem of course is that habits, routines and disciplines are hard to establish, tough to do regularly and can be really hard to keep going.

During the Covid pandemic lockdown, lots of people in the UK did a daily workout with the fitness expert Joe Wicks. He, overnight, became the nation's PE teacher. He was great. But over the weeks, the viewing numbers fell, people stopped doing it daily and the viewers gradually started to get smaller, and eventually it stopped.

Why? Well, people discovered sourdough bread-making, and the videos were a bit of a fad, a temporary thing. Nothing wrong with that, not everything we do is permanent. I don't drink mulled wine in June. Most though, to be honest, just did not establish a sufficient habit, routine or discipline. The same happens every year with new year resolutions. I have spoken about this on the radio on January 1st. Why are gyms full the first few weeks in January but are back to normal by February 1st? People don't have a big enough 'why', and they do not establish a sustainable habit.

The book *Atomic Habits* by James Clear has sold millions of copies. People are obviously keen to stop bad habits and take on better ones. That is not in dispute. It is encouraging too. In the book he mentions a few key things which are worth further study and investigation. I love how he emphasises ease and the obvious. He says to establish a new habit we should 'Make It Obvious', 'Make It Attractive', 'Make It Easy', and 'Make It Satisfying'.

Even establishing a new habit requires routines and disciplines. Having as little friction in front of a new habit as possible is one of the keys, Clear states. Say we wanted to start jogging. Something as small as 'I don't have any running clothes clean' is enough to stop us dead in our tracks in the early days. But on the flip side, washing and putting out some jogging clothes beforehand is enough to get us out there more often.

Even little practical things like that can help us to keep on going.

Grit

Dealing with the grit in our lives or the stone in our shoe, if you like, can make us more persistence-focused.

I think its fair to say I'm not a great car mechanic. My idea of a great car is one that works when I start it and gets me to my speaking gigs on time. If it is clean that's even better, but that is not a deal-breaker – I have had small kids.

So when my sister called me for some help with her car years back, I wasn't very excited to be honest. "It's making an horrendous noise Lee, can you come and have a look at it?"

So I popped round to my Mum's house where my sister was staying, and got in her car. It was unbelievable! As I drove six feet there was a scraping noise that the whole street heard, worse than ten nails scraping down an old-fashioned school chalkboard. As I tried to turn the car around it got even worse, I thought it was going to fall apart at any second!

So, I rang my friend Derek the retired mechanic, held the phone to the car wheels and asked him to diagnose it. He said, "It's the brakes Lee, I reckon they could be seized or they are in real trouble, but if you drive it the brakes might overheat and they could explode".

"Er, I think I'll leave it then Derek, thanks."

So we called the breakdown van and got the car removed to a local garage. When it arrived at the garage, it was lowered down over the inspection pit. But when they looked at the brakes there was nothing there. No problems and no noise at all.

I couldn't believe it, my sister and my niece had had to shelve their plans and had to stay with us for an extra night with a baby, and for what?

A piece of grit. Yup, a piece of grit had got wedged between the brake pads and discs.

This tiny piece of grit had ruined my sister's day and involved seven other people to get it fixed. Apparently, as the car had rolled off the back of the recovery van, the grit had become dislodged and then disappeared without a trace.

It's amazing that this tiny piece of grit had had so much impact on our lives. It would have cost my sister over £400 to get recovered to her home, if it hadn't dislodged.

Our grit.

Some families haven't spoken for decades because of an argument that no-one can even remember.

Some people stay in a job they hate because they once failed an interview.

Some people were once told as a kid that they were worthless, and they've lived their whole lives believing it.

Small pieces of grit (some are easily dislodged; some take much longer), can have a massive impact on our lives. If you think small things don't make a difference, then you've obviously never slept in a room with a mosquito.[41]

Sometimes we can survive and thrive a whole lot better by checking for our own 'pieces of grit' which may be lodged in our thoughts, beliefs, actions and attitudes.

Have you ever reflected on what could, or has, stopped you from keeping on going?

What holds you back in yourself?

What words spoken over you are you holding onto that simply aren't true?

We aren't a boat designed for the harbour; we are designed to be on the open sea, going places, connecting with others, making a living, making a difference.

Unresolved life grit makes its mark and persuades us that we are destined for pootling around the harbour, never setting sail for the bigger life.

41 Attributed to the Dalai Lama XIV or as an "African proverb"

Work/life balance

Struggling to get find the perfect work/life balance?

I believe that there is a reason for that. It doesn't exist. I think it is a myth.

Work/life balance is something that we should consider, as many work too hard, but we can learn about it on a course, we then try and do it when we leave and we can end up thinking about it all the time.

Personally I think it's unachievable if we are going for perfection here. There is always a trade-off between work/life/family etc. I think if we are not careful it's something we can always be seeking and always feel like we've failed on. So it can become a burden.

Seasons

I prefer thinking about seasons.

I believe in seasons, I think it's healthier and easier to balance.

Every job is different, but they often ebb and flow. Maybe we have a season of busyness at work, and then a season where it quietens down a bit. We may have a season of work events and a season of deadlines/budgets/appraisals etc.At home, maybe a new puppy, or a season of focusing a lot on one member of our family, when they are struggling, or even have a wedding coming up, and then a season where they don't need as much help anymore.

Life and work is in seasons. So one of the key reflections to do is stopping for a moment and asking "what season am I in right now?".

Tell your family that in the run up to a big event or season. "I'm going to be busier than normal this week, but I'll be around on Saturday, let's go to the park".

You'll have to do some long hours. But it is a season, and hopefully it won't last forever.

Stress and burnout is complex but it can be exacerbated when seasons last too long or when we don't make the proper adjustments in our schedules or in our approach or mindset. It is sometimes that we are in the wrong job of course, a toxic workplace is just that, toxic. But still, seasons will come and go, change and pass.

When the first hard Covid lockdown had passed, we moved into partial lockdown, and I felt a real change in the season.

Not all seasons are for harvesting though, in our instant gratification-obsessed society we want it all now, but sometimes we need to be resting, planting, nurturing, and growing. And it is because of those seasons we will reap the rewards of our efforts later.

What season are you in? Ask yourself regularly. Remind yourself that no season lasts forever. And that time off is part of the ebb and flow too.

Recognise the season, communicate with your loved ones, make the adjustments, be kind to yourself.

The 'After 8' rule

I'm a comedy fan. I watch it online, on TV and live too. I've even been on five comedy courses now and I've done some stand-up myself. As a speaker you'd think that it would be easy for me, but actually stand-up is very different to being a speaker. One of my mates, who's a full-time comedian, was joking with me that quite often speakers and even vicars chat to him saying, "We do the same job really, don't we?" I think he probably doesn't say anything, but to be really honest they are very different. Stand-up comedy is like speaking on speed and it is often cited as one of the toughest things we can do. Well – it's not brain surgery or defusing bombs, but it is pretty tough. It is scary because, not only are people generally scared of public speaking, but add to the mix that for stand-up the audience are sat there expecting that you'll make them laugh every 10-20 seconds. When I'm speaking I aim for a laugh every 3-5 minutes, every 20 seconds is hardcore.

Lots of people I've done comedy with are doing it to build their confidence and to push themselves out of their comfort zone. Our comfort zone is great, but we grow when we push ourselves out of it, like getting a new job or trying something new for the first time. As a speaker I just wanted to push myself to be better 'in the moment, on stage' and so stand-up comedy/improv courses are one of the few places I can go to stretch myself. Lots of people try stand-up, lots of people fail – there is a high drop-out rate, almost as high as the drop-out rate at the gym on the third week of January. So when people really make it in comedy, I like to find out more and learn a bit about their story.

Sarah Millican is one of the big names in comedy right now. She has been on a long journey to get there. My friend, who has run comedy nights for years, said that Sarah slept on his sofa years ago as she did the local circuit, learning her craft.

Being from the north-east of England myself, I've always liked to watch north-eastern comedians, and when Sarah Millican hit the big time I thought she was great. She is cheeky, thoughtful and honest. As I started following her on Twitter I saw some articles about her. For example, she does an amazing thing every Christmas helping lonely people by using the hashtag #joinin to encourage people on Twitter to support each other at a tough time of year for many. Brilliant.

In the first Covid lockdown I went every week to Sarah's online comedy gigs. It was like an oasis in my week. I and a few others were also often chosen as the front row people too (ie we were on the zoom screen and allowed to laugh, not just in a remote audience). We had such fun over the months as she built a little community of comedy fans. I got to know Sarah, her husband Gary and the hosts a little too as they heckled me (mainly because of my job title of course!).

But one of the things that I discovered about Sarah, could well be one of the secrets to her success. She calls it 'Millican's Law'. She developed this during long runs on the Edinburgh Fringe where she was doing dozens of comedy gigs back to back.

So, here it is...

If Sarah has had a bad gig, she only allows herself to be mad, moan, wallow and be angry until 11am the next day. Then she draws a line under it and gets on with the next gig. Because if she goes into a new gig thinking she's terrible then, of course, she'll probably fail again.

But there is another side to it too

Even if she nails it, storms it, does well or gets a standing ovation. She only allows herself to be smug until 11am the next day too. Then she draws a line under it and gets on with the next gig. Because, she says that if she goes into a new gig thinking she is God's gift to comedy, she'll lose her sharpness and her focus and she'll probably fail.

She says that this little law has made a real difference to her. It has helped her move on from life's ups and downs.

But because Sarah is a comedian and they live fairly nocturnal lives, getting home in the early hours and getting up late, then 11am works for her. But for the many of us who have day jobs, we might need to move that forward to 8am.

So Millican's Law has henceforth, in my head, become the 'After 8' rule. Yesterday was yesterday, and whether it was a bad day or a good day, today is a new day, with new opportunities.

Don't live in the past, embrace the present and learn to move on.

8pm

PS If you want to go even deeper on this, then no matter how busy you are, if you work roughly office hours, you might be tempted to use your phone, tablet or laptop in the evening.

If you clocked off at 5pm, make sure you do clock off, and I'd encourage you to switch off your devices, after 8pm.

There's no point having to deal with something at midnight, and it be on your mind and you can't sleep. So, think about switching off your devices and leaving them in another room. Switching off email is good for us. We are not supposed to be 'on' 24/7 and notifications are not our friend.

New day after 8am. Switch off after 8pm.

Buy some time-related wafer-thin mint chocolates to remind you, and treat yourself with one when you actually do it!

Rest is a weapon

Rest is a weapon for the 'battle' – and maybe an underused, misunderstood and underrated one too.

Good sleep is one of the key ways to help us keep on going. Bear in mind that sleep deprivation is used as a torture technique in war, so its importance should not be understated. It is the equivalent of powering down or restarting your brain after a busy day.

A lot of hidden things are happening in our brain when we sleep, there is a rewiring and a flushing of waste taking place, amongst others. It is good for us. I remember when we had twin babies, and at times were desperate for more sleep, we'd walk past bed shops and just stop and stare longingly through the window at the comfy bed and white fluffy pillows, like a hungry stray dog looking through a butcher's window.

But beyond sleep, we should start to prioritise rest if we want to 'fight' for longer. In recent years people have become more and more interested in some ancient practices such as a 'sabbath'. Whether it is a secular or sacred sabbath is up to you, of course, but nonetheless a day or part of a day off every week goes a long way in topping up our reserves.

Do you have a day off every week? Do you regularly unplug from the plugged in world that we live in? It is not good to be connected all the time.

Disconnect daily for a few minutes, weekly for a whole day if you can, and some would also say disconnect and rest monthly for a weekend and annually for a whole week. After resting, judge how you feel the next week.

Rest is our fuel for the journey. Self-care is good as I've mentioned but it is only one step. We can, and for our own wellbeing should go deeper.

Look again at your workload, look again at when you disconnect, look again at when and how you take breaks and a holiday. If you were away from your phone (but family could still find you in an emergency), would you do it for more than an hour or two? How would you feel?

Stopping is hard for some of us though but it is worth it. Those who do not stop at all are sometimes doing it deliberately, or because they know no better.

Slowing down makes us dive deeper, it can bring things up, but that is all part of the process, we can't run forever. Don't use busyness as a shield from meeting yourself. People often ask me, "Been busy?" I know they often mean well, but I just don't see it as a sign of success.

My hope is that you will start to enjoy rest and some deliberate laziness. All in the name of wellbeing and resilience! We give out so much in the week, we need to have a day of input too. Silence, solitude, stillness, sabbath and slowing are all a part of the resilience toolkit.

There are myriad reasons why we don't always prioritise our own rest. All rational, everyday reasons.

- "I have a busy job"
- "I have kids"
- "I have to care for my Mum and Dad"
- "I rarely get a break"

- "How am I meant to do this?"

However, understanding that rest is a weapon is all about starting the journey, because – trust me – the quieter day never comes, we have to make it happen.

'Ave a break

Most of us just have to look at our schedule, the moments we have. First, we should look at the time we spend on screens. Many people who tell me they are 'time poor', can and do spend six to eight hours a day on their phones.

Sometimes, as I travel, I see people having quick breaks from their jobs. Some are having a quick smoke or a tea, some are chatting, but most are stood outside the back door of their workplace on their phones. We often don't even queue anymore without being glued to our phones, with the views of everyone in the world shouting at us.

We are not supposed to hear the world's opinions on every subject over our short smoke or coffee breaks. Realising that rest is a weapon starts with something as simple as choosing not to open our phone in a supermarket queue, or closing our eyes and resting instead of reading 20 social media posts on our seven-minute work break. It is not good for us to always be giving out, or always listening to others views.

One of my aims is to work on a life that is as full as I want it to be, but with space to enjoy the moments and deal with the tricky stuff as it happens. To be honest, I am pretty much an activist and a pragmatist, I like doing stuff and I love solving problems. I am often busy, but now I feel the call to rest more than before – it has got under my skin because I know it is good for me. We treasure our quiet Friday nights and Saturday mornings and strolls in local parks.

Also, over the years we've also tried once a year to go our favourite place – Lindisfarne in Northumberland. One of the reasons we go there is that it is a tidal island, so when the tide is in we are cut off and we have to slow down. It is deliberate and enforced rest for us, we spend a few days reading, watching good TV, walking slowly, watching seals and generally being windswept and interesting. It makes me slow down. I find that helpful, so I keep doing it.

The 80/20 margin

A good measure of this all is to aim to be 80% busy, but leaving 20% as a margin for rest and 'life'. Even farmers know this trick, they don't harvest the whole field, they leave a margin, and also they leave a field to rest too.

Some people I know are, or they tell me that they are, 100% busy. Fair enough, that is their choice, but then when something out of the ordinary happens like a broken-down car, a work or family emergency, then they can't handle it because they have no margin to play with.

Keep a healthy margin.

We should try to work from a place of rest because rest is a weapon for us to use. Let our rest be the the fuel for a more balanced, resilient and fulfilling life.

As the old adage goes: 'If your output exceeds your input – then your upkeep will be your downfall'.

A more balanced approach

"Nothing in this world can take the place of persistence. Talent will not: nothing is more common than unsuccessful men with talent. Genius will not; unrewarded genius is almost a proverb. Education will not: the world is full of educated derelicts. Persistence and determination alone are omnipotent."
(Calvin Coolidge, the 30th US President 1923-29)

Great advice. But I think it should also say: press on, rest – press on, take good advice, push through, rest – be accountable, press on, rest – push through, have a break – press on, have a good old laugh – press on etc.

QUICK WINS

Sharing for success

We should all aim to share our life, our dreams and our struggles with at least one person – even better, a trusted handful of people that you see regularly.

But don't over-share these things. Over-sharing can be as bad as under-sharing.

Under-sharing can lead to serious mental health issues, over-sharing can keep us going around in circles and bathing in the bad stuff, never seeing a way out. Even with professional help.

It's a fine balance to achieve but a good one to attempt.

Obstacles, friction and mistakes

Some people spend their whole lives trying to remove life obstacles for themselves or their children, but maybe they are missing the point.

Hollywood star Gwyneth Paltrow was being interviewed and she shared something quite remarkable. She shared that her philosophy on fame is that it is actually not very good for us as people, because everybody famous starts to remove all of life's obstacles, and she said that it is the friction caused by those obstacles that is what makes us grow.

It reminded me of this moment in music between the jazz legends Miles Davis and Herbie Hancock. You can view the story here: https://youtu.be/m6fVZtp9vGQ or search for it online.

In 1963, Miles Davis was playing one of his famous long trumpet solos and Herbie Hancock, a much younger musician, played a wrong chord. He was mortified. But Miles heard the bum chord, stopped for a second and then started to play a series of notes that incorporated that wrong chord and he started to riff on it, saving both the solo and Herbie's blushes. He was able to make something out of a mistake, an obstacle. That moment was key in Hancock's life and work, realising that he can make good of something that did not go well.

"... what I realise now is that Miles didn't hear it as a mistake. He heard it as something that happened, just an event and he dealt with it... and since he didn't hear it as a mistake, he felt it was his responsibility to find something that fit and he was able to do that. That taught me a very big lesson...the important thing is that we grow and the only way we can grow is to have a mind that's open enough to be able to experience situations as they are and turn poison into medicine. Take whatever situation you have, and make something constructive happen with it..."

Team effort

"Resilience is not rare, we all have it."

Dr Samantha Boardman is the author of many books on the subject of resilience. During the Covid lockdown she posted regular videos on her social media; in one of these she reminded her viewers that resilience is the norm, not the exception. She went on to encourage us that it is more of a muscle we can build and develop.

We all have muscles. We all have resilience.

Dr Boardman quoted a researcher – "Resilience isn't easy, but WE can do it." The important thing here is the 'we'. In my experience, people often talk about self-care as the only thing we need.

If people are struggling, they rightly talk about self-care, particularly if they have been super-busy or are on the edge of burnout. But the 'we' should not be skipped here. Accepting and giving support is really important for our wellbeing too. Helping and connecting with others builds our resilience. Self-care is so important, but it is only one part of the whole resilience picture, maybe even just the first step.

Find your person of peace

One of the things I do in an audience, online or offline, is to look for what I call the 'person of peace'. I look for someone in the audience who nods their head, looks interested and smiles. If there are two or three of those people, I'll concentrate a bit on them rather than the uninterested grumpy person that appears to be elsewhere.

I won't stare at them, but I'll look at them, notice them and then I'll come back to them especially if they are enjoying it. These wonderful people in life, work and audiences get you through. As much as I like reaching and engaging the grumpy people (because I like a challenge), I have learned to focus more on the people of peace.

Who is the person of peace in your life and at work?

You don't have to tell them they do that, but do occasionally thank them for being encouraging. I am so grateful for the handful of people who encourage me in different parts of my life.

In my book here, as I can give them a copy, I'd like to thank my two friends called Joan –Joan Ibbotson and Joan Freeman. They are people of peace for me. Great encouragers.

Have a seat

Sitzfleisch is one of those amazing German words which has no English equivalent; it literally means 'sitting meat' or 'sitting flesh'.

It is not a comment on our bottom. It is more about the ability to sit still and focus for a long time, showing 'sitting still' stamina and the focus to see a task get done.

In the working world in Germany, having sitzfleisch is considered positive feedback, saying that you have the ability to concentrate and complete things well.[42] 'Staying power' or 'endurance' is another way of describing it. We all need to develop this, whether at work or even watching a long concert. It is underrated. We all need breaks and our productivity does dip over time, but if we can develop the ability to produce well while being seated it is a useful thing.

What rhythm of standing, sitting, walking and being focused works for you?

---

42 My German friends tell me that it can be used as a word to describe family or visitors who stay in your house a bit too long too!

Yes or No

One phrase I have always loved is, "Let your yes be yes and your no be no".

So much time is spent not telling people a straight answer to their requests. It is important to be kind and good to others, but that also means tell them the truth about arrangements or requests.

If someone asks you to do something and you can't, or you don't want to do it – what do you say?

If someone asks me to help them and I can't, I now say, "Sorry, I can't", rather than saying yes and letting them down or hoping they don't come back to me.

Let your yes be yes, let your no be no. It may be slightly more awkward at times and it does require more assertiveness from us, but it makes life a whole lot simpler to manage. No guilt, no drama, and don't get on the shame train - just a yes or a polite no. It makes life simpler.

Subo

I love to show people the audition video of the singer Susan Boyle from *Britain's Got Talent* in 2009. It used to be one of the most viewed videos on YouTube.

The reason I show that video to talk about Susan Boyle's story is because, in the interview before she she sang, Ant or Dec asked her: "Have you been singing long?" And she said, "Since the age of 12."

Everyone forgets that part of her story.

We like the rags-to-riches story that 'Subo' was a woman from a little village in Scotland, and now she's a multi-platinum selling artist, but we forget that she sang in her kitchen, her bedroom, in the local pub, and in the church choir for years and years before she got discovered.

Sure, she found fame at the age of 47, but she had been singing almost her whole life.

Let's just agree once and for all that there's no such thing as an overnight success.

Creating a regular routine for success

Daily

Before you dive into your email (which is basically someone else's task list for you) stop and think - what do I need to do today - before anything else?

Regularly reward yourself - get outside, step away from your desk or workplace.

Weekly

Stop and check on your progress for key things.

This is what I need to do by the end of the week……..

This what I need to do to nudge this forward………

At the end of the week

Reflect on what you've done/achieved/moved forward - and tell someone who will understand and be happy for you.

- Write a quick to do list for next week.
- Take a moment to take it in.
- Remember its about progress, NOT perfection.
- Then close your office/laptop/van/shop and walk away.

Big life laundry

Sometimes we have to do a quick check. We have to press pause and take stock.

Most of us have to work to pay the bills. We do of course sometimes work to serve others, to get ahead or move up – our motivations can be mixed. But in my experience, be careful with the money thing.

We sometimes choose money over time. If we are not careful, we can end up working very hard for people we don't like, in a job we hate, just to buy things we don't need and won't make us happy. Don't sacrifice your long-term health and wellbeing to fuel a financial decision. There is no point buying a bigger house, a newer car, or a nicer kitchen if we have to burn ourselves out to do it.

When making financial decisions take into consideration your time, family, stress levels, workload capability and wellbeing too. Some jobs are really hard, I understand that, but honestly, I have seen some really stressed-out people at times who could be a whole lot less stressed-out, if they just adjusted their lifestyle a little.

Pringles®

I was getting a bit stressed about our Christmas arrangements one year. You know how it gets - who is arriving when, and who is leaving at this time or that time, whose house are we going to, the sleeping arrangements - the meals out and the meals in etc etc. Ah the joys of family Christmases.

My friend Andy was listening to me very patiently and he eventually said: "To be honest, as long as there are Pringles® I'm happy wherever I am".

He was right. I stopped trying to control and understand all the complex arrangements, I just needed to be present when I needed to be and yes, I went out and bought some Pringles®.

The beef ones, of course.

Christmas was great. The Pringles® were pretty good too.

Feed yourself - become a lifelong learner

There has never been a better time to learn. Ebooks, audiobooks, podcasts, videos, book-summarising services, and lots of other ways to learn are available 24/7. We have no excuse now not to learn regularly. Even if you're not a big reader and you don't particularly like books, you can still listen and learn in many different ways.

Learn new things every day and – as they say – let every day be a schoolday. No matter what your schooldays were like, don't let them remove the joy of learning.

One of the best things about my job is that I pretty much have to learn. I love to learn and then I put that stuff into practice or point other people towards the stuff I've been learning. Or sometimes I just learn for the fun of it and gather information in museums or by asking people stuff.

Just make sure your media intake diet is balanced with good learning and balanced learning, as there is so much misinformation out there.

Be careful of the echo chamber too, only learning about things or seeking opinions you agree with; the YouTube rabbit hole can run dark and deep. But even so, occasionally read and listen to things you don't agree with because it sharpens you up.

Enjoy learning, it is good to increase your input.

Get Good® at gratitude

In all the research I have done and things I have looked at over the years, much of which I mention or occasionally debunk in this book, there is a good thing that stands out from the crowd as both helpful and proven.

One thing that benefits us all, and helps us to keep on going is gratitude. Being thankful.

Years ago I read an article[43] in a national newspaper where a journalist who was (rightly) very cynical about most of the famous 'positive thinking, no matter what' type of self-help books that have sold millions, was surprised and it seemed, a little embarrassed to admit that he had been keeping a gratitude journal for almost a year and it had a real positive effect on his state of mind.

I love it when people are genuinely surprised and then write about these things slightly embarrassed, it takes real guts and integrity.

Practising gratitude on a regular basis will make a positive difference to your state of mind. It is well researched even just from the article in the footnotes.

43 https://www.theguardian.com/lifeandstyle/2009/aug/15/oliver-burkeman-happy

Take a few minutes out and write three to five things that you are grateful for in a nice new notebook. You might want to put them onto a scraps of paper and put them in big jar like I have seen people do. You might want to blog about them or record a video or even use an app.

Interestingly, it doesn't have to be everyday – that can be counter-productive and a bind. Just do it regularly and find the right time of day for you.

Eventually this way of seeing 'the good stuff in the tough stuff' while looking at life does become embedded in your lifestyle and moulds itself into a good habit.

Abundant gratefulness is a sign of flourishing. Those who regularly say thank you have their eyes looking outward and upward rather than unhealthily inward.

I think being grateful is successful because it takes the focus off ourselves.

This is a good thing. However you choose to be more thankful and grateful for the little and big things in life, give it a go, like the journalist did.

If you are not sure, just review it after a few weeks and notice what difference it makes.

Doubt

The NBA superstar Kobe Bryant once said in an interview: "Doubt is such a strange thing. There'll be times when you succeed and times when you fail. So wasting your time doubting whether you are successful or not is pointless."

It is.

"You just put one foot in front of the other. You control what you can control and then you see what the outcome is.

If you win, great, you're going to have to wake up the next day and do the journey over again. If you lose, it sucks but you have to wake up the next day and do the journey over again anyway."

What other people think of me is none of my business

Sounds harsh, but actually it is a good boundary to develop.

Worrying about what the world may, or may not, think, or say, about us is a road to nowhere.

All people are valuable, but not everyone's opinion of us is of equal value.

Create for wellbeing

Become a creator, not just a consumer.

Do something creative, make something, have fun, be creative. Don't worry, no one has to see it, it doesn't have to be public or go online. Just withdraw from the busyness occasionally and create something new.

Groundhog Day

In January last year, I for no apparent reason, got a bit stressed-out and miserable. Then my wife and I realised we had nothing in the diary to look forward to.

We talked about a short February break and also about going to New York later in the year. We both felt so much better after having something to look forward to in the diary, I remember an almost an immediate change in my mood.

As the ancient proverb goes: "Hope deferred makes the heart sick".

Check your diary and make sure you have something to look forward to in there.

It doesn't have to be something expensive but just something you'd enjoy, a change, a visit, a day trip, a party, a meal – a break from *Groundhog Day*.

Practice doesn't make perfect...

...but it is essential for success.

Don't give up practising what you need to practise.

It will probably be boring. It may feel pointless.

But you will need it for success. And the experience it gives you, you will use in the future.

Tough day?

If you're having a tough day just slow down and press pause for a moment and read this slowly…

Did you know that you are unique?

You are special, you are amazing.

Did you know that there is no one in the world that has your fingerprint, that has the same retina, or has the same voice pattern, that has the same DNA?

Even my identical twins and they don't share any of that stuff because even though they are identical - they are unique.

That means that you bring something unique and special to the world that you live in, the family that you're in and to the workplace where you work.

No one can bring what you bring.

So, when you are having a challenging day, be encouraged.

You're unique, and you are bringing something amazing to this world.

You are special.

Enjoy that.

Get out

Many studies have shown that going outside and connecting with nature is good for us. We knew this centuries ago, but now it is even being prescribed by doctors. Why? Because it is well researched.

If I am not careful, I can be in my office facing my computer all day without connecting with the outside world. I know that even in the middle of a busy time I sometimes just need to get outside, no matter what the temperature is.

In the strict Covid lockdown the sale of dogs went through the roof – sometimes for people to have something to do, sometimes for company, but also because it gave people a reason to go outside. When we were only allowed outside for one hour a day here in the UK, dogs were everywhere. Interestingly, the government knew the importance of exercise and nature too. They never locked us up 24 hours a day, they encouraged us to go outside into nature even with the virus around and no vaccine, because for us, as a nation, not going out would be very bad. Don't forget to connect, not only with other people but with nature too.

Back in my youthwork days I remember taking a group of urban teenagers to the countryside for a residential holiday. On a walk they stopped on top of a hill and were almost blown away by the really strong wind. I realised that they had never experienced a strong wind on a hilltop before. Their faces were a picture; they loved it, they felt connected.

Belief vs truth

Something doesn't have to be true for it to be a big belief.

When someone thinks something for long enough it eventually becomes a solidly held belief.

This belief is usually not true.

We often need to believe and trust ourselves a bit more.

We need to stop repeating and believing the lies we sometimes think.

Högertrafikomläggningen (aka Dagen H)

On the 3rd September 1967, Sweden decided to do something radical. They decided to stop driving on the left and started driving on the right-hand side of the road.

Can you imagine that?

That Sunday they just did it. They mobilised loads of volunteers who were pointing cars in the right direction. Can you imagine the chaos on the roads when it happened?

That was one of the biggest changes a country could make. A little decision with a big impact, but they made it, and with only a few minor accidents too. The photo went viral when it was rediscovered.

The way that we approach change is a way that we become more resilient. The person with the most flexibility will have the better outcome. I really believe that, and as I get older, I don't want to be stuck in my ways, maybe I will be with some music tastes, but I want to be someone who's open to changes, and I want to be someone who is flexible enough so that I can deal with life's changes along the way.

A few months ago I was tested! This is what I wrote down on the day.

"I was all set up on Zoom this morning for my day of presentation skills with 14 leaders and as I said hello I heard a loud 'pop' in my office and all the electricity went off. I managed to get the Zoom which was now running on my laptop battery onto my phone internet. Then we moved all my stuff into my dining room and I continued after a short break where the delegates introduced themselves. Phew.

Then at the break time I rang the electrician and he was ready to come round so I removed all the stuff from the top shelf fuse box cupboard and dropped a cough mixture bottle onto the kitchen floor, and it smashed everywhere – on my shoes and all up my shirt! My Mam came in and cleaned it up while I continued with the training with my stinking but strangely clearing cough mixture shirt on! I eventually found and fixed the issue in the office and hopefully it'll be OK tomorrow when I buy a new extension lead. I'm grateful for my wife and my Mam – all in all, what could have been a disastrous day turned out OK. Phew. PS if anyone knows how to get cough mixture off a wooden floor, feel free to tell me."

I was partly prepared for disaster (with my phone backup wifi), but also I got some help and I thankfully was flexible enough to make some changes and carry on. It was an odd mixture of panic and peace at that moment.

Things may well change to give us some kind of peace, but life will always send us other things to deal with. Managing ourselves well is the ability to find peace in the storm. When the sea is turbulent on top, it is peaceful deep down.

Brain bandwidth

Our brains are amazing, but they aren't infinite or unlimited, particularly when we are 'in the moment' – doing things.

When you are going to a new place in the car, have you ever turned down the radio when you get near so you don't miss the turning?

When someone asks you something and you are walking, do you stop or slow down?

If a family member asks you a question, do you stop stirring your tea?

These are funny little experiences, but really helpful when it comes to understanding our brains.

We were having a lot building work done at our house a few years back and it took months, always longer than you thought it would. I was working at home most days unless I was at an event and so was around when the builders were there. After a few weeks, I noticed that I was becoming much more indecisive. I thought – what is going on? So I asked my friend who is a psychologist and he told me I had 'decision fatigue'. And the penny dropped, I had been answering small and insignificant questions for weeks several times a day.

"How many sockets do you want on this wall?"

"How many shelfs brackets do you want to use?"

"What shade of off-white do you want this wall?"

"Do you want USBs on these sockets Lee?"

After a few weeks I had no opinion on, or interest in socket placement! It was relentless. I realised that my brain or mental bandwidth was full. To be honest, I went to work to do a speaking event for a break. I remember feeling quite similar when my twins were toddlers. My friend just nodded, he had hit the nail on the head.

Sometimes our brain is fresh and alive, other times, particularly at times of stress or pressure, it feels kind of full.

If you live in a busy house in a built-up area, your wifi router will be working hard, and at certain times it will slow down. I see a drop in speed when the schools close and the students arrive home, or in the evening when everyone gets back and starts streaming movies or playing online games. The broadband bandwidth is taken; there is less space. So, can we make our brain 'bandwidth' bigger? Can we train it? In a word, no. But we can do some practical things to help recover some bandwidth.

Getting enough sleep is the big one, but also we can delegate more, say no to things, realise that we can't do everything, we can write to-do lists and notes (I do this a lot) because at least it gets the info out of my brain until a later date. Get into nature or focus on something else, maybe by writing about your day. Or just never have any builders in your house. That might work too.

Find the ways that work for you to free up your brain's bandwidth, as sometimes we need to be ready to make bigger decisions with enough cognitive processing power to make the right choice.

The real pro

One of the most powerful forces in the world is maybe a tsunami, a hurricane, a typhoon, maybe it's gravity, or as someone once said to me, maybe it is love. All great answers, but here's what I think is one of the most powerful forces at work in our lives though… procrastination. Some of us are so good at it that we put the pro into procrastination, if there was an Olympic sport, we'd probably win a gold medal. We all do it. I often get people to put their hands up in a big crowd and admit if they're procrastinator. Almost all hands go up. Everyone is, or has been a procrastinator. If you can deal with procrastination, you'll find that work is so much better.

In Armenia, in 2010, they built the world's biggest single chocolate bar[44], weighing 9,702 lb. There are pictures of it online. Many others have tried to beat it since. It's real chocolate and it was massive, even though it looked a bit like metal or plastic. As a chocolate fan I really wanted to know how they ate it. There's a photo, and you see the guy who made it, with a big tray and a meat cleaver, and he's chopping away, taking bits of the chocolate off. He handed it out to the local towns and villages nearby.

That's how we beat procrastination. That's how we keep on going with a big task – we chop stuff into smaller pieces, manageable and achievable pieces.

Procrastination really kicks in when something looks too big. Our brain freezes and we don't say we can't or won't do it - then we suddenly start getting interested in other things and start doing odd things, like tidying up or putting things into alphabetical order. A procrastination red flag.

If something in life or work looks too big, just like the guy who distributed the world's biggest chocolate bar, chop it up into smaller pieces. Then it seems more manageable and our brain will kick back in and help us do what we need to do. Consultants and logistics experts get paid big money to basically chop big projects into more manageable pieces.

When I used to help students with revision, I'd always tell them to not put 'science' on a revision planner as it is too big. I got them to focus it down into smaller subjects: science-physics-light refraction etc.

Once it is made smaller, that is when the work gets done.

---

44 https://www.sandiegouniontribune.com/sdut-armenia-produces-worlds-biggest-chocolate-bar-2010sep11-story.html

How to Keep On Going through anxiety

Everyone has felt anxiety.

Some live with it for a fleeting moment, some for a season; others live with it most of their life.

When I reflected on the anxiety I have felt at various moments and seasons of my life, and the hundreds of people I have helped with their presentation anxiety, I realised the crossover between my worlds as researcher/speaker on motivation and wellbeing and as a presentation coach – probably a third of which has become me helping people with their anxieties.

Here are some of the tips and tricks I have used and taught delegates over the years as I have helped them to manage their anxieties around presenting.

Firstly – clarification – I am not a qualified psychiatrist or psychologist and I am not diagnosing or commenting on serious medically diagnosed clinical anxiety here. Although you will, of course, see the similarities, as public speaking is one of the biggest things that activates people's anxiety. I imagine public speaking like a bank of buttons that get pushed: buttons of self-esteem, self-worth, imposterism, values, past history and also hurt. No wonder it is so hard for many, and becomes a phobia for some.

Imagining failure

Seth Godin gets it spot on, I reckon, when he says, "Non-clinical anxiety is experiencing failure in advance."[45]

Anxiety is often imagining ourselves failing. In the context of presenting, it's imagining all the horrendous things that could happen. People use the expression, "I might die on stage". Not many people die on stage. Comedy legends Eric Morecambe and Tommy Cooper did, but it's a very rare thing. Not many people die on stage; some people fall off a stage occasionally. For some people, it doesn't go quite as well as they want it to, but not very few people die. But it's funny the language that we use.

Anxiety, if we don't deal with it, can grow. A relative of mine lost their best friend a few years ago. With no warning, he killed himself. It's not something that we should ignore.

If we don't recognise it for what it is, and learn to handle it, it's something that can take over our lives, it can stop us doing things. It can even make us make bad decisions. A friend of mine, who also coaches speaking skills, told me their client literally smashed their car into a wall the morning of a work talk to get out of delivering the presentation. They didn't go 100 miles an hour, but they deliberately crashed their car, so they could ring up and say, "I've crashed my car, so I can't make it."

I had a client who told me that they moved jobs, because they realised that their job was going to involve presenting. They changed role just because the social anxiety was too much. They didn't go for any promotions, because they never wanted to present. Their anxiety around presenting became such a big thing, like someone who has a big fear of flying and so never goes abroad. That's when it starts to really affect our life, that's when it becomes a problem – and that's why we need to deal with it.

Just call it what it is and start talking about it to others.

My friend Steve McDermott says it's about, "Getting into THE right state, not A right state." (This phase sounds much better with a Yorkshire accent, by the way.)

45 https://seths.blog/2013/08/the-opposite-of-anxiety/

Most of our anxieties can be reduced through state management: the state of our brain, the state of our emotions, etc.

If we manage our state we perform better. NLP[46] and CBT do lots of this work. That's why we see Olympic athletes wearing headphones before a big race, and why Usain Bolt spent 25 minutes before his big races walking around and high five-ing the crowd – he was warming up his body and his mind, he was managing his state. Everyone was pleased to see his fist-bumping, his high fives, he even said hello to the volunteers and officials. He was doing that while running up and down, managing his state so he could be optimistic, focused and prepared for the race. It was all state management stuff.

I've seen this a lot with top swimmers too. They'll come out in their tracksuit with their headphones on, and then weirdly have to get undressed in public. The very last thing they do is take their headphones off and put them in the box, and then they dive into the pool a few seconds later. Maybe they are listening to their favourite songs to get into the zone, they might be even listening to their coach or themselves in their ear saying, "You can do this", "You've got this", "You've done it before, do it again". They're listening to block out the critical voices, maybe their thoughts of feeling like an imposter. They are doing something very practical to manage their state.

Music and words can be very powerful to manage our anxieties. In 2019 there was a photo released of the tennis player Serena Williams sitting on the court during a break, reading some notes. She later revealed that she reads the seemingly scrappy little notes often; she writes these herself when she needs an extra push or when she wants to re-focus in

46 NLP = Neuro-linguistic programming - the controversial but very commonly used set of ideas/concepts and pseudoscience theories developed in the 70s. See my note about eating the meat and spitting out the bones! See: https://www.quora.com/Is-NLP-Neuro-linguistic-Programming-a-pseudoscience
CBT = Cognitive behavioural therapy, a taking therapy dedicated to helping people to turn down the volume of their critical voice and it teaches coping skills: https://www.mind.org.uk/information-support/drugs-and-treatments/talking-therapy-and-counselling/cognitive-behavioural-therapy-cbt/
The excellent book *SUMO* by Paul McGee makes CBT very digestible and is put into plain language.

mid-match.[47]

Going back to the presentation anxiety analogy: if we're 'ready to rock' – maybe a little apprehensive, but we're ready – that's good anxiety. Being wracked with nerves, panicking and wanting to run is not. I have always loved Christmas, and I remember as a kid, coming downstairs on Christmas morning with my sister, feeling a bit nervous wondering whether Santa had been. That wasn't bad anxiety, but there was an anxiety there: a nice nervous.[48]

That's the difference. We can sometimes tweak our anxiety from the feelings of dread to: 'I've got this', 'I can do this', 'It'll be OK'.

It's a helpful way of reframing things. It takes work, but it is worth it.

The big fight – a little bit of neuroscience

There's a fight that takes place in our brain. This fight is between the limbic system[49], and the little part of our brain called the amygdala, and our much larger prefrontal cortex. Our anxieties live mainly in the amygdala, very close to our brainstem. So it's nothing complex. It's the basic stuff – it is our fight or flight mechanism. It's designed that when a tiger is running towards us, we think, do I run away from the tiger or do I punch it in the face? That's what the amygdala is saying to us. It is very simple. It is black or white, there are no greys.

How many people act like this? Like that person who crashed the car to get out of presenting, how many people want to run away when they have to present or do something big? We want to get out of there, we want to run away. I once had someone on my speaking course who really struggled and the organiser eventually took them out, because they literally wanted to run away. I could see that their brain was screaming

47 https://www.thesun.co.uk/sport/tennis/9470884/serena-williams-secret-notes-wimbledon-alison-riske/

48 Again, a nice analogy I picked up from my friend Steve McDermott. Probably a throwaway comment he made that I remembered from years ago.

49 Sometimes wrongly named as the reptilian or lizard brain, based on early 1960s neuroscience by Paul McClean.

at them "get out!" Once they'd walked around the building a few times, they got that out of the system, they came back in and they were able to deliver. Their amygdala kicked in - they wanted to leave the room, they wanted to flight, they desperately needed to get out.

There's no negotiating with the amygdala, it is fight, flight or freeze. It doesn't do complicated.

What can really help is to move our nagging anxieties from our annoyingly very basic amygdala into our prefrontal cortex. It is one of the last parts of our brain ready to develop at the front area of our brain. This is why children and teenagers are not very rational: because this part of their brain is still in development.

I think of the prefrontal cortex as the BBC Radio 4 part of our brain. Where we can think, "Hmm, let's just reflect on that. Will I really die when I am speaking in public?" "Probably not, Lee, so let's do it then shall we, my good chap?"

It is much more polite and rational. It can deal with grey areas, it can deal with complications and nuances, whereas the amygdala can't. "Public speaking? Nah Lee, that is scary stuff, you might die or be embarrassed for the rest of your life, leave it alone. Let's run, hide and talk to no-one."

One of the things I think works well is to get our brain to try and rationalise the fears. Ask some questions that will trick and help your brain to get out of the 'fight or flight' loop – the bit when we want to go to the loo, again! Our palms are sweaty, we can start to think the worst, "I know nothing", "I am not experienced enough", "I am not good at this", "They'll all hate me". These are all anxious, amygdala-type thoughts, intrusive, annoying and easily believed. If we can grab and nudge these thoughts to the more rational part of our brain, we can start to think differently.

Don't believe everything you think

We have to believe some things that we think, but if I believed everything I thought, I'd never get out of bed in the morning.

Paul Simon, one of my favourite artists, was interviewed and they asked him, do you ever get writer's block? And Simon, one of the most prolific musicians and writers of all time, said, "No, not really – writer's block is just listening too much to my critical voice.' He has chosen not to.

Writer's block says everything we write is rubbish – so don't write anything. Paul Simon said he had found a way around it, and he has kept writing and producing many albums and big projects.

Have you ever had your drive or garden paved at home? They put down a black membrane before they start to lay the paving to stop the vegetation growing through. Otherwise we just end up getting grass and plants coming through the paving. There is a drive near me that did not get this put down, and I see big weeds growing when I drive past.

I think of our anxiety voice, our critical voice, being like that membrane – it stops the creativity from coming through. Stops us having fun. Stops us from fulfilling who we are and why we are here. If we continue to listen to our critical voice, we won't be able to do very much and certainly won't be able to live and work with any kind of confidence.

I wonder how many work and creative projects the critical voice has stopped over the years? How many companies and charities weren't formed - how much art was not made, how many albums lay on a dusty hard drive or reel to reel tape in a cupboard somewhere?

Lies lies lies

I can't remember the number of nervous speakers I have worked with who tell me all morning long that they are rubbish at speaking and then storm it in the afternoon when it is their turn to deliver.

Their anxiety was leaking out of them. It does leak out. Sometimes it spills out.

One of the annoying things about anxiety is that it feels very real. Most of the time, it's not – it's only perceived reality. It's the stuff that we're making up in our heads.

These thoughts are known as ANTs by psychologists.

Automatic **N**egative **T**houghts.

Some estimates say we have 6,200 thoughts a day and some even say that 80% or more of those are negative. It is our brain telling us about threat and fears; it is part of our natural survival mechanism. But these thoughts can get skewed and feel very real. We can be pessimistic, ruminate, catastrophise, and become perfectionists (more on that shortly).

We can be swimming in our anxious thoughts. Swimming in treacle.

So how can we help ourselves be less affected by these ANTs?

One of the best ways to deal with them is to ask questions, to get ourselves out of our head into the real world. For instance, if you are about to present, ask yourself, 'How long have I been in my job?' It is a good question to ask.

'Do I know anything about what I am about to speak about?'

Hopefully, you won't be speaking about stuff you don't know anything about, so that one is easy usually.

Something around our experience is a great question to ask ourselves to silence the ANTs. If I start getting a bit nervous, maybe before a big keynote presentation, one of the questions I'll ask myself is:

"Lee, have you ever done a talk before?"

A crazy question to ask, right? I've literally done hundreds. It's been my life.

"So, Lee, have you ever done a talk before?"

"Yes."

"So shut up, and get on with it!"

That's how tough I am with my occasional presentation anxieties. I tell my brain to quieten down, replace the ANTs with more helpful thoughts and questions and then crack on, as we say here in Yorkshire.

I might also ask:

"Have I got anything to say?"

"Have I written a book about it?"

"Have I got any relevant content for these people?"

"How many times have I delivered this kind of stuff?"

"Hundreds of times, so get on with it, Lee - –and chuffin' enjoy it!"

I think we need to be careful.

We shouldn't mollycoddle our anxieties. We can pander to them if we are not careful.

We can easily accept, repeat and believe the perceived reality that our brain has cooked up.

We should treat these thoughts as the imposters they are. I encourage my speaker clients to frame it in a way that says something like "I am just here to share my experience and my expertise." [50]

For presenting, if you needed some advice you'd seek out an expert. We are often experts in our field. But somehow anxiety means that we tell ourselves that we know nothing at all. And so we imagine ourselves as

50 Or even "my fresh perspective"

a little baby presenting at the front of a room of adults. That's why we've got to have a little word with ourselves to get out of our head and into the real world.

Stop now and write down some questions that you can ask yourself when the negative thoughts and anxieties turn up.

No one has to see these questions - but do write them down. Be ready to douse the fire of the ANTs.

The danger of trying to be perfect

One of the other problems that can make us unhappy and less resilient is that annoying, but recurring visitor – perfectionism.

It can visit us, out of the blue and without warning. I think we've all been at least a bit of a perfectionist at some point in our lives.

Maybe we are very relaxed about stuff in general, but sometimes we can be, weirdly perfectionist about strange things like putting up Christmas decorations: "Oh, no, that's just slightly to the left and I need to move it – it's not quite in the middle". Same for rug placement, picture hanging, slide design, window cleaning, mowing the lawn etc – most of us have our odd little triggers in this area. We can write a report and proofread it 100 times just to check that the spelling is correct.

People do think it is good to be perfect - so they aim for a 10 out of 10 on everything. If we aim for 10 out of 10, we'll always fail. Lower the bar.

Wait, hang on. Er, Lee, aren't you supposed to be a motivational speaker? Are you telling me to lower the bar?

Absolutely I am.

Because 7, 8 or 9 out of 10, is enough. No one achieves 10 out of 10 on any task.

I've done hundreds of talks. Trust me, no one is 10 out of 10. I've never been able to achieve 10 out of 10; I'll always skip a word or mispronounce something. Maybe something I say won't quite land like I thought it would, but I'll carry on and it'll be fine.

On my absolute very best day, with the perfect audience and with the wind behind me, I might be a 9.9 out of 10 speaker. But even if I was - if I'm not careful, perfectionism anxiety will focus on the 0.1 that wasn't perfect.

Aim for progress, not perfection. It should always be about progress - never about perfection.

Be kind to yourself. Perfectionism is the opposite of that.

Ask yourself after a task or project 'did I try my best?'

Don't ask yourself, 'Was it perfect?' Because if you do, you'll just start that cycle of anxiety once again and your joy will be stolen by the fiery ANTs.

Ask yourself, "Did I try my best?"

Learning from the King

Fancy a good film tonight? Go watch *The King's Speech*. It's a great film. The film shows King George VI getting more and more anxious, which in turn affects his stammer, because he's trying to be word-perfect, like he thought his Dad was. He idolised his father, King George V, as a great orator, and he thought he could never be that good and so his speech got worse and worse, to the point that he couldn't really do public speaking very much at all. So he went to get some help.

The story is funny, endearing and heartwarming, it's a nice film to watch. But if you watch it you through the eyes of presentation anxiety, it takes on a new depth. I've never been word-perfect in my life. I'm okay with that. I'd rather be authentic and engaging than word-perfect and robotic.

Back to habits, routines and disciplines...

Better routines are a proven way to keep our everyday anxieties muted, or at least at a lower volume. In the same way that we have to keep half an eye on our bodies by watching our food and drink intake[51], we also have to work on our wellbeing and mental heath. If we don't have some good habits, routines and disciplines in place, it will go downhill, like our bodies will too if we are not careful.

Knowledge is great, education is key, but we need those habits, routines and disciplines or we are doomed to failure and life will not change for us.

If we are anxious presenting, or in other life situations, we need a new habit, a new routine, a new discipline to help us.

I often ask nervous presenters, what's your-pre talk routine? Have you ever thought about that? If you think you don't have one, you still have one, you just don't know that you have one.

An anxious presenter's pre-talk routine may be completely unknown to them, but it may still be faulty.

In practice, your boss comes to you one day and says: "Could you present at this conference for me next week?"

And you say looking at them: "Ah, er well, erm yeah, er okay then, I guess."

Gulp.

Then you text your best friend: "I've just been asked to present next week, I hate presenting."

They respond straight away: "Ah yeah, I hate presenting too".

Then you text another friend: "I've got a presentation next week, I hate it".

And they say: "Yeah, I hate it as well. It's not for me. Ever".

Then you start a WhatsApp group with eight of your friends called 'We all hate presenting' and you all share your own historical stories about how you all hate presenting and how someone at work once dried up and started to cry during a talk. And before you know it, you've started this whole thing – you've pushed a tiny snowball off the top of a hill, and the snowball is rolling down the hill, getting bigger and bigger, collecting

51 I don't mean dieting here – I mean, it is not good to get up at 9am and drink ten pints of beer. We all make sensible choices, and some not-so-sensible ones, every day.

snow, negativity and ANTs as it rolls down. It grows, along with your anxieties.

Think about the routines you have:

- How do you look after your body?
- How do you look after your state of mind?
- What makes you feel more or less anxious?

Adapt your life routines. Get help when you need it. Become accountable for your routines and actions to good friends.

Breaking news

You'll know, I'm sure that one of the quickest ways to get rid of some general anxiety is to stop bathing in the constant negative news feeds we have on TV and on socials.

I watch, listen and read the news. A bit.

But I limit the bad news that I consume because, if I watched it all the time, I'd get too invested, probably angry about what could be done. It is not good for me.

It is called breaking news because it is breaking us.

I can't solve all of the world's problems. I can only control the controllables.

I can't control what happens in Westminster or the White House. I'd like to - but I can't. I can vote once every four or five years. I can write to my MP, be part of a local political party even, but I can't control what happens nationally or internationally on a daily basis.

The news, dressed up as 'I want to stay informed and up to date', ultimately makes us feel powerless. There's no point us watching or reading the news all day long because we can't control it.

It chips away at our mental health. It feeds our anxieties.

It can make us angry at the world too, as it slowly starts to skew our view of people - making us think that everyone in the world is corrupt, dodgy or suffering.

This is far from the truth. Most people are just trying to get on with life carving out a living and are usually good or neutral, reading some news sites, you'd think everyone in the world is a criminal.

Routines

As many before me have said in many contexts – learn to control the controllable. One of the biggest things we can control is our routine.

So if your boss says asks you to do a presentation - say to them: "Sure, I'll give it a go". Not, "Yes, brilliant, I will smash it, and of course be perfect". And not, "I hate presentations".

Just, "OK, yeah. I'll give it a go. I'll take some time out this week to have a think about that."

There and then, you have already started a better, more positive and healthier routine. You have pushed a smaller and way less stickier snowball off the top of the hill.

Ask yourself a few questions a couple of days before, have you got your preparation done? Have you got your stuff ready? The night before, have you eaten properly? Have you put out the clothes that you're going to wear the next day? Have you got your notes and your laptop and your props or anything else you need? Have you put it all by the front door?

I put all my stuff by my front door, so that in the morning, I don't have to think. Mornings are not my most lively part of the day, so I adjust my routine to make an allowance for this. In the morning, I want to get up, not really think about it too much, put the clothes on that I've put out, including my shoes, my wallet, and my phone. I want everything to be there.

So I just pick it all up, I grab my bag, my coat, my phone, my wallet, car keys, box of props then I go out and I can deliver what I need to do. I don't want to be stressed in the morning thinking, "What am I going to wear? What am I going to do?"

Taking his lead from Albert Einstein, President Barack Obama only had two suits. I mean, he had lots of them, sure, but he only had a grey suit and a blue suit to choose from. Also one style of shirt, one brand of underwear and one brand of socks and shoes. The only decision as President of the United States that he had to make in the morning was, is it the grey or the blue today? He only changed what he wore after he stopped being President, because he knew when leading the western world that his brain was kind of full, and he just didn't want to have to decide what he was going to wear that day.

So when your brain is full of anxiety, simplify your life, get a good routine, eat well, get your breakfast, make sure you get up on time, do what you need to do, get everything you need and get out there.

And as comedian Troy Hawke says "Shoulders back and smash it".

Brew more of what you love

The negative stuff in life can stick to us like a very sticky thing.[52] So maybe we need to get some positive stuff to stick to us too.

Eg if someone has given you some feedback on a talk, and it was nice feedback, write it down. Collect that stuff. No one has to see it, just you. So that before a talk, you can look at this feedback to spur you on.

I've got loads of notes on my phone. Notes on different things in life, shopping lists, talk and book ideas etc. But I've also got a note on my phone that I can use at the back of a room just before I am about to get on stage. I can read it quietly, and I don't tell anyone about this. I shouldn't be telling you really – cheeky. I just read it to myself. It's emails and testimonials from clients. It's the things that people have said to me after I presented. If I read that before I present, it doesn't make me arrogant, far from it. It just helps me to be confident and in the moment, knowing that I'm the right person at the right time and in the right place.

52 I wanted to use a brand name here but I can't. You know the one I mean – it is very sticky, it has a rough side and a smooth side and is often used as a fastener in coats and kids shoes and rhythms with 'hell no' – like their legal department's reaction to using their name.

There is of course a very fine line between confidence and arrogance; I try to stay firmly on the right side of that line, or my audiences and my family will throw things at me.

If a colleague says to you, 'well done - that was a good presentation'. Or 'I enjoyed that'. We can easily bat these kind of compliments away. We wave our hand embarrassedly - that gesture can be like batting the positive and reality away. 'It was nothing', we say, walking on and forgetting all about it in the busyness of life. What we should do is say, 'thank you' and then quietly write it down and keep it.

This could be the most exciting part of the book for some. I am encouraging you to buy more stationery!

Get yourself a nice new notebook. I'm giving you permission to buy stationery. Exciting times.

The only thing you can write in that notebook, though, is positive things that people have said about you, your work or (if you do them) your presentations. Then you have a little resource to fill, a little resource to draw on when you need that encouragement. I use my phone more now, but I still use notebooks too.

Take that notebook everywhere you go and watch it grow. Just remember to add to it regularly. Brew more of what you love.

A reflection of my own

...on excellence, ego, me, my job and how I keep on going. Reflect on your own job as you read this.

I believe in excellence. Absolutely. And I want to be the best presenter I can be. But what I realised, particularly as a professional, is that if I'm not careful, that quest becomes egotistical.

I'm there for the audience. I'm not there for myself.

You can see this sometimes when people speak in public. They just tip over into ego mode. It becomes more about them than about the audience.

One of the worst presentations I ever saw was from someone a bit rich and a bit famous off TV (no names!) who basically told the audience about how brilliant they were for 30 minutes and then sat down.

The audience just collectively shrugged at the end, because it was all about the speaker, not about helping them, the audience. It was a business audience and they were waiting for some business solutions and insights and all they got was the persons CV. It was so dull.

So for me, it's reminding myself of, and knowing that I'm there for, the audience. I'm there to draw something out of them. I'm there to help them and shine a light on something that will change their world. So, because making a difference is a motivator for me, I tell myself I'm there to make a difference.

I'm there to help them. That helps me to relax.

If I say I'm the world's expert at something, then it becomes about me, not about them. Understanding who the audience is and why I am there helps me to relax and enjoy it.

One delegate asked me recently in a Q&A if I ever have the fear of not being liked. Of course, it's nice to be liked, isn't it? I want to be liked a bit – most people do – but I've learned that if that is too heavy audiences don't like it. Audiences are always split. I think they're split into 20-60-20. 20% of the audience will love me. 60% will think I'm OK. The other 20% might think, I don't like this guy. They won't like my dress sense, my accent or my demeanour.

I'm okay with that. I bear these stats in mind.

When I am travelling back after doing a talk, I can have a happy journey knowing that a few people connected with me and my message, but – more importantly – knowing that my self-esteem isn't too affected by what people think of me when I visit their workplace for a few hours.

Can you re-read the above and replace my reflections with your job, life or situation?

Up in lights

Recently at Christmas, in Leeds city centre in Yorkshire, they made the poem by Kate Ryrie into brilliantly lit up words that spanned the biggest shopping street in the city. They looked stunning, and people stopped to read them as they shopped.

They, for me, sum up many people's experience in life and are a helpful reminder that no one is without their history, hurt or anxieties…

So with butterflies in our bellies, step into the limelight.

Whatever your limelight may be, you may well have butterflies, but as I have heard many times: "It's all right to have butterflies in your stomach. Just get them to fly in formation."[53]

It's not all cuddly toys and sweetie shops. Our feelings do not always line up how we want them to.

Looking back, some of my best life and work experiences have been when I am out of my comfort zone and feeling a bit out of my depth but sorted my head out enough to dive in anyway.[54]

53 Attributed to many people inc. Dr Gilbert

54 Once literally, as I stage-dived into the crowd to end our gig at a music festival. It was the thing to do in 90's hip-hop I think.

Control the controllables – then give up the illusion of control.

Life is not controllable, that is one of its joys.

My version of this popular tool might help:

get good®
at LIFE

The Get Good Target

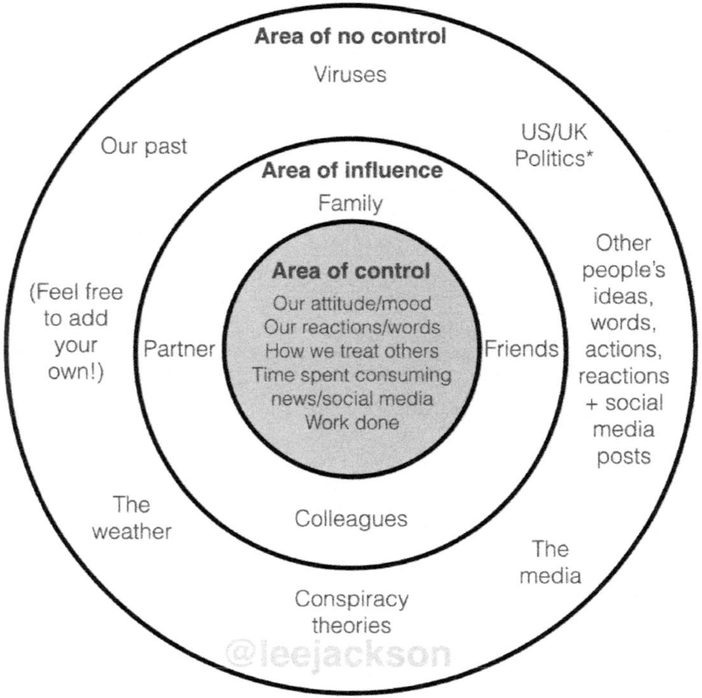

Derived and adapted from many sources inc. the work of Steven Covey and Stoicism

*Please note: this doesn't mean that you shouldn't vote or be involved in politics, it is more about where you spend a lot of your time or what 'brain space' you hand over to these things.

"A cheerful heart is good medicine"

Ancient Proverb

And finally…

…don't take yourself too seriously

There was a great social media thread about an overly serious local football team, when a guy enquired about playing a bit of five-a-side one night a week. What he got back was a 14-page epistle to read. It was only for an hour on a Wednesday evening, but he got back an essay and a rulebook. Someone was obviously taking their role as the five-a-side pitch booker way too seriously and this post started a great thread of people's experience with individuals and organisations taking themselves just a little bit too seriously.

Ironically, my industry does lean towards the 'let's take ourselves very seriously' side of things. I always think that kind of misses the point of self-help and personal development, but often intensity comes from trying to do the right thing and forever digging deeper into our motives etc.

Yes, I do take my job seriously, because delivering talks, training and writing is a great responsibility, but I do work hard not to take myself too seriously.

Why wouldn't I?

"Because not being serious might harm your brand, Lee."

I think it enhances my so-called brand, and to be honest I don't want to work with people who are very very serious and have no sense of humour anyway. Unless they need this help of course.

Even those in the toughest jobs in the darkest coalface industries tend to have a sense of humour which becomes part and parcel of their coping strategy.

At the height of the Covid epidemic, I was quietly told of a group of medical staff who, after clocking off from work on a 'hot' restricted Covid ward, would have a quick socially-distanced beer after their shift to relax and unwind. They took off their PPE and shared a chilled bottle of beer – but not just any beer, they used to only drink Corona beer. I can imagine them lifting up the cold beer, seeing the word 'Corona' and being thankful for another day on earth.

Developing our humour chops and looking for the lighter side of life, not taking ourselves too seriously, is a genuine strategy to survive and thrive in today's society. I've met lots of great people but quite a few overly intense ones too. The stress is dripping off them. The last thing in the world I'd do, by the way, is to say, "Hey lighten up". It's a horrible thing to do, almost as bad as shouting, "Cheer up – might never happen, mate", to someone as they are walking home from a friend's funeral. Always a recipe for embarrassment or worse. But I do sometimes wish that the very serious people would occasionally take a step back and see that a lighter touch on life works wonders.

It is a strategy, a lifestyle option. There is so much good in raising a smile.

I was attending a comedy course in a local church hall one night and we were doing warm-up games – you know the type of thing: word games while passing them around the circle making each other laugh etc. Halfway through, a man in bare feet and yoga pants came storming down and angrily barked at us, asking us to be quiet because he was trying to "relax his clients". You know when you know you shouldn't laugh, but then you laugh more because you shouldn't laugh? Yeah, that happened, big time. Bless him, sure, we were a bit too loud, but his angry bare-footed stomping while trying to tell us he was teaching 'calm' made it all the more funny.

Sometimes sharing our day with family and friends helps to de-stress. A few years ago I went to the opticians to get some new glasses, and hardly any of the frames on display would fit me. I learnt in this process that glasses have width measurements, so I looked for these width numbers and made my choice. I shared with my optician about the issue of having only a few to choose from, and as he was cleaning the lens and not facing me he said the immortal words, "Yes, you do have a large cranium Mr Jackson". I wasn't quite sure how to respond, sat there with his lens contraption stuck to my face, he'd just said in his posh and eloquent way that I had a really big head.

Hashtag rude.

When I got home I told my family - they loved it and it is now a phrase they use often when they want to wind me up.

I went to the audiologist a few months later too and he told me that I had very small ear canals! So now I officially have a big head and small ears – they might need to change the Mr Potatohead toy.

I could get het up about these comments from trained, learned medical professionals, or I can just smile and tell people about them.

I chose the latter. Everything is content in my job.

The multi-award winning country music star Reba McIntyre said, "In order to be successful, we need a wishbone, a backbone and a funny bone".

I love that quote, we need to have a dream, a goal, a vision, whatever you want to call it. We also need to have a backbone, to learn how to keep on going, but I love the fact that she says we should have a funny bone too.

When I meet someone who takes themselves really seriously, it really stands out to me now, it's like a stone in my shoe, a wrinkle in me undies. I will continue to learn to laugh at myself and to try to hold things lightly. It's good for me, it's good for my wellbeing, my health, and actually it is good for my clients that they know that I'm serious about my work, but I don't take myself too seriously.[55]

I had to tweak my onstage intro too, as a speaker, to sound more like me and less like a list of accolades. It is always good to give the host or MC a written intro to set up my talk, otherwise they might say anything – or often they cut and paste from my website and it is way too long. These intros are traditionally often just a list of achievements and job titles. But I like to write them as short intros to my talk, why I might be helpful and who I am but without making it sound like I am super-serious.

They often go a bit like this:

"Our next guest today is an award-winning motivational speaker, author and a past President of the Professional Speaking Association. He works helping people to Get Good in challenging times. He's from Leeds, but don't let that put you off. Please welcome Lee Jackson…"

55 Large organisations hardly ever have humour at their heart, but in Scotland they did us proud when they got the public to rename their gritter trucks. These boring but vital lorries that keep the roads open now have great names including… Buzz IceClear, Spready Mercury, Bear Chills, Gritney Spears, William Wall-Ice, Snow Connery and many more!

Then I find that people get a hint that I have something to say, I have some relevant experience but I might be more approachable and authentic. It certainly helps to get the audience on my side as we learn together. Tweaking your intro is just an example of how you can be more comfortable in your own skin.

Being more confident in ourselves often helps us to be more relaxed. I remember how hard it was starting the couple of careers that I have had. The first couple of years were hard work, learning, adjusting and finding my feet. But as I have gotten more experience I certainly relax more. Right now I will speak to any audience of any seniority, anywhere in the world. What you see is what you get. Professional, but not too serious, because it is not all about me, it is all about others: my audiences, connections, clients and colleagues. I want less of my ego and anxieties and more of my best self who is comfortable to not take myself too seriously.

As author Donna Ashworth, reminds us, don't think only about your looks, they are never going to last, but let your sense of humour mature like a fine wine. The more seriously we take yourselves, the unhappier we're going to be.

Failure

The other way we can take ourselves too seriously is when we have made mistakes or embarrassed ourselves.

Fundamentally this is when we think that we are the only person in the world that has ever made a mistake. We think no one in the world has been that stupid. No one has ever done that or everyone is perfect. Sometimes we can think randomly about the times that we've embarrassed ourself in front of others or made a mistake and, if we are not careful, we can take that very seriously.

When I teach presentation skills people often ask me about humour and how you insert that into a talk. The best and safest kind of humour and the safest is self-deprecating humour – having a little bit of a go at ourselves and not taking ourselves very seriously. Comedians make a living doing this and, as long as it doesn't go too far and becomes a self-esteem crisis, it is usually a good thing to do.

Years ago when I was doing a talk at a conference, somebody heckled me and said that I look a little bit like the 1980s UK TV presenter Keith Chegwin. Everybody laughed including me. Sadly Keith is not with us anymore, but he is a fond memory for many and when they see that I look a little bit like him it's funny, I get a laugh and the audience then receives the message that I'm a speaker who doesn't take himself too seriously. So I use that joke now because it's fun, it's self-deprecating and as time passes I can also make the joke that if they know who Keith Chegwin is, they must be over the age of 40. Some speakers I have seen wouldn't do a joke like that and would not compare themselves to somebody who is a light-hearted figure of fun. I don't mind.

If we take ourselves and our mistakes very seriously, it's bad for us and we can come across as aloof and cold to people as well. I love helping audiences to relax and to break the ice in an appropriate way. This skill is a tricky one, because it can be used badly and inappropriately, like I'm sure you've seen at lots of work events or conferences. There is safety in laughing at ourselves and yes, it is good for us. As a couple, my wife and I have occasionally left places, meetings or meals and not been quite sure why it all felt a bit odd. Usually it is when someone is very, very intense or, frankly, if their personality type doesn't help them to relax.

I am passionate and intense at times, we all are, but I am also fully aware that in me, like most people, there is a little bit of Alan Partridge, David Brent or Michael Scott waiting to pop to the surface. These comedy characters work because we can see ourselves and others in them. Mostly, they mean well – they just get in their own way, don't read the room, overshare or lack self-awareness.

To get good, we'd better get good at getting bad!

Failure is a part of our success and development. We can get annoyed at ourselves but, if we can hold our successes AND failures a little bit lighter it is good for us and those around us. I played a game of basketball recently and I played pretty badly, and I was not a happy bunny. Then I realised that I was in the middle of writing this chapter and I had a word with myself. The day after, I got some nice comments about the game and stats too. I hadn't lit up the scoreboard, but actually we had done alright against a tough team. My failure was mainly in my head. So now I can bear this in mind for next time.

UK national treasure, the actor Judi Dench ('M' in the Bond films), has won it all on stage and screen, She has been a great example of holding her success and failures well. In recent interviews in her advancing years, she is reflective, self-deprecating, funny and grateful. She smiles embarrassingly when people tell her she's a national treasure. She seems to holds all that stuff very lightly. Her glittering awards including her Oscar® are just standing in a normal-looking cupboard in her living room. Also, she has a door mat that reads, 'I've been expecting you Mr. Bond'. I like that.

Bobby

I called my comedian friend Paul 'Silky' White and told him I am writing a chapter on not taking yourself too seriously.

He said, "Perfect timing, I have just been talking to a dog called Bobby about croissants!". He sent me this photo of the dog, Bobby.

Silky sums it up well. Be interactive, explore, go with the flow, look for funny moments to lighten yours and others day. Because, as he reminded me - we will find what we look for.

If we look for bad stuff or bad people we will find them, if we look for death and corruption it will be there, but if we look for fun, interaction and humour we will also find that.

We can have either a negative or

positive confirmation bias in our mind, to the world and ourselves too.

No one is perfect and life can be hard. Let's enjoy and laugh at our imperfections and the bumps we hit along the road. Not everything is a disaster, we are not failures, we just occasionally fail.

That's ok. You'll be ok.

Enjoy the journey.

Look for the light

Don't deny the darkness
But look for the light
The small chinks of light
The glimmers of hope
The funny things we notice
The quirky people we meet
Those times of real connection
The loved ones we see
It doesn't take a floodlight to extinguish the darkness
A small candle will do that
Look for the light

Printed in Great Britain
by Amazon

24884493R00116